MW00623040

"One of my favorite nice guys has gone rogue, which is pastoral talk for telling the truth. It is good to see the congenial Sandy Mason walk on the wild side. He has decided to say what so many want to say, but won't - that much of church work has little to do with serving Christ. Sandy is a rare combination of intellect and grace, a gifted preacher with a prophetic note. His work is simple, but it cuts to the quick and you hardly notice you have been told off. There are many writers who wax eloquent, who soar through celestial galaxies, yet don't really know what they are talking about. Pastor Mason is living his words, he has taken on the grandest of all tasks, being a disciple and making other disciples in the local church."

- Bill Hull, Author of *Christlike: The Pursuit of Uncomplicated Obedience*

Smarter than Jesus?

Sandy Mason

Smarter than Jesus?

Published by:
Intermedia Publishing Group, Inc.
P.O. Box 2825
Peoria, Arizona 85380
www.intermediapub.com

ISBN 978-1-935529-66-8

Table of Contents

Dedication   I

Acknowledgements   III

Introduction   V

Chapter 1:   1
Calling Brings Clarity and Confidence

Chapter 2:   21
Preaching is Not Passé

Chapter 3:   41
Praying is the work of the Ministry

Chapter 4:   61
Disciple Making and the Power of One

Chapter 5:   83
Spiritual Warfare is a Path to Freedom

Chapter 6:   103
Spiritual Disciplines, The Pathway to Renewal

Chapter 7:   129
Evangelism Rarely Happens in the Church Pew

Dedication

This is the easiest part of the book to write. Without question, God's greatest gift to me has been my wife and ministry partner, Margie. Her love and confidence in me has called out the best stuff in this pastor. Honey, I never could have done this without you!

Love,
Sandy

Introduction

Acknowledgements

West Kenyon, for his wonderful cover design
and creative and technical insights.

Judi Roe, for her meticulous and thorough editing
of the early editions. She made it better!

Larry Davis, Terry Whalin and the Intermedia team for
their patience in bringing this project to completion.

The Desert View Bible Church family, for living out
the message of this book with me.

Introduction

Introduction

Thus says the Lord, stand by the ways and see and ask for the ancient paths, where the good way is, and walk in it; and you will find rest for your souls. - Jeremiah 6:16

Obsolete! Have you ever felt obsolete? Pastors today may feel about as obsolete as Hummer salesmen—relics of a bygone era, irrelevant to where the culture is going. If we are to believe all that is being written by her critics, the day of the local church is long past as we await something more relational, individual and hip. Some are content to "fellowship" through their computer, attending an electronic service while never leaving their home. The more sophisticated and well-heeled Christians find commitment to a local congregation confining and mundane, preferring to seek a broader range of experiences and connections. No question, the Church is her own worst enemy, famous for being slow to change and notoriously behind the times in methodology. Are we just moving around the deck chairs on the Titanic?

Any student of church history knows that the Church of Jesus Christ has experienced regular seasons of ebb and flow: good times when the Church boomed with growth, evangelistic zeal and love of the Scriptures; and darker times when attendance on Sunday bowed to the bar scene and righteousness and justice were just wishful thinking. No doubt, the Church in the western world is currently in such a season of dissipation and retreat. Net church growth is

> *No doubt, the Church in the western world is currently in such a season of dissipation and retreat. Net church growth is down, and the generation under age forty in the United States is becoming an unreached people group by missiological standards.*

down, and the generation under age forty in the United States is becoming an unreached people group by missiological standards.

What are our options? Pack it in and hope that our African and Asian brethren will come to rescue us? Re-invent the local church as a coffee house and hand out inspirational tracts with the vanilla latte? Or get back to the original blueprint for ministry and evangelism as modeled for us in the life of Jesus?

As a pastor with over twenty five years experience in both mega-churches and new start-ups, I found myself needing to write a map for my next ten to fifteen years of ministry. I have been in the fight long enough to see the fads come and go, to see what really lasts over the long haul in the lives of people, and to see the carnage of broken pastors and their families who with all good intentions ran their ship into the rocks of an insatiable consumer culture—in the church.

Once highly-motivated believers, now tired of the busyness of life in the local church, claim to be "burnt-out" and retreat to the sidelines. What had begun as their passion and joy has become a burden of begging volunteers to sustain programs and services for an increasingly apathetic congregation. Their bookshelves at home are full of notebooks from the latest seminar that promised to bring life to their thirsty souls and increase attendance and momentum in their churches.

Perhaps your soul resonates with what I am describing. All the special events, must-see concerts and latest seminars of the Christian community have you feeling tired and longing for something simpler and more profound. The local church you lead or attend is trying hard to market itself to the community with the best of intentions, but with the unexpected result that the core leaders are busier and more harried than ever. All the while, a creeping suspicion lingers in the back of your mind that you are flailing away at the branches and not getting to the root of the issue in people's lives.

I developed a mantra for the first three years of our church that many of these folks found frustrating: "Crawl, walk and run."

The desire for programs and activity is rampant in our culture! When I started our church plant here in Phoenix, I was amazed at the level of expectation from Christians regarding their pet program: "When are we going to get it up and running?!" I developed a mantra for the first three years of our church that many of these folks found frustrating: "Crawl, walk and run."

For the first couple of years we learned to crawl, focusing on the basics of worship, relationship building and small groups. While many of our people were refreshed by the simplicity and clarity of what we were about, the activity addicts moved on, complaining that we didn't have enough ministries in place to suit them.

Underlying this desire for more activities for our families is a world-view that is theologically flawed. A subtle shift has occurred in where we place our hope, as if it is all up to us! To grow and sustain the church, that pastor or church leader must create the right atmosphere: Contemporary worship and dynamic message, gourmet coffee and the coolest kid's building. Who can stand under the crushing weight of such expectations?

Like the Old West Sheriff who lives in constant fear that a faster gun will ride into town, the modern church leader worries that the new church down the block will franchise Starbucks or build a mini-Magic Kingdom to lure their consumer-oriented families away. What's worse, we have really come to believe that we are in competition with the world's ability to entertain, a game we are sure to lose and only makes us look more shallow and foolish to the discerning seeker.

Jesus was not competing with the Vanity Fair of His day. He was a prophetic and intriguing alternative to the emptiness of what the world offered. As we will explore in chapter 7, there is an inherent danger in using the bait of the world to draw people to Jesus. They develop a taste for trite.

Our practice belies our theology. We may claim to believe Jesus meant what He said to Peter in Matthew 16:18: *Upon this rock I will build My church; and the gates of Hades will not overpower it.* But our frenetic level of activity and heavy emphasis on attracting the mildly curious shout loudly that the future of the church is really all on us. It is too much to bear. I can imagine Jesus wringing His hands and cheering us all on from the bleachers, hoping we will do this church thing right so we don't lose the next generation!

Thus says the Lord, stand by the ways and see and ask for the ancient paths, where the good way is, and walk in it; and you will find rest for your souls. (Jeremiah 6:16)

It is time to go back to the ancient paths, the good way of Jeremiah's prophecy, that we might find rest for our soul and for our congregations. That rest comes from knowing we are doing the important things: the work God has called us to do, the ministry that will nurture the life of Jesus in the hearts of our people and change the landscape of our communities.

There is a problem with this ancient way, to be sure. It is slow, it requires endurance and courage, and it will not be applauded by the spirit of the age. In fact, you will find resistance in your own head, and in your own well-trained instincts to feed the beast and bow to the insatiable appetite for success in numbers and influence. But, as many of our brothers and sisters have discovered, if you feed this beast for long, eventually it will devour you.

Jesus' invitation in Mathew 11 to do it His way still stands: *Come to me, all who are weary and heavy-laden, and I will give you rest. Take my yoke upon you and learn from Me, for I am gentle and humble in heart, and **you will find rest for your souls.*** Note that He is quoting from our key scripture, Jeremiah 6:16.

This is Jesus' word for church leaders of the Gospel today, the same word Jeremiah called the servants of God to in his day. The tragic response of the people of Judah to this impassioned call is recorded at the end of Jeremiah 6:16: *But they said, 'We will not walk in it.'* This is always our challenge. Will we listen to the passing priorities of men or to the timeless Word of God?

The irony of our generation is that we have amazing technology to follow one another's every step and to record our every thought on an electronic billboard—but we are less and less skilled at sustaining real relationships, real intimacy. Technology cannot help us be more human. We need the wisdom of the ancients for that. So it is in ministry.

It is the natural course of things that the next generation questions what they have inherited, and rightly so. We should sift the chaff from the wheat of past methodologies and keep what is essential. My concern is that we not lose sight of the essentials as demonstrated in the life of Jesus. Methods come and go, but the essentials of ministry are the building blocks of the Kingdom. We cannot neglect them and expect to build a ministry of lasting influence, of real fruit.

A favorite methodology of churches to reach new people is the "fall festival." Here we substitute a family-friendly and mildly Christian event as an alternative to Halloween. We offer free hot dogs, live music, a balloon contortionist, inflatable playgrounds and live animals in a petting zoo. By doing so, we attract people to our church that would pull into a parking lot on Saturday for free food and the chance to pet a goat! Just the sort of raw material we're looking for, right?

I invite you to consider the methodology and philosophy of the ministry of Jesus Christ, particularly as revealed in the Gospel of Mark.

As a church planter, I have found Mark's Gospel to be Jesus' roadmap for launching a new work of God and sustaining it. As we have humbly sought to do what Jesus did in planting our church, our congregation has experienced the same kind of opposition and blessing that marked the ministry of Jesus. In fact, it would appear that every lasting work of God in church history has been marked by these same priorities.

As a church planter, I have found Mark's Gospel to be Jesus' roadmap for launching a new work of God and sustaining it.

The question really is this—which generation are you serving? If you only want to "make your mark" in your time, to impress your peers and satisfy your ego, you can find a variety of strategies and literature to accomplish that goal. There are very human ways to draw a crowd that work just as well on Sunday morning as they do on Saturday night downtown. Get the right music, the right website, a good communicator with humor and a propensity to self-reveal, and people will show up.

But if your calling is to bear fruit that will last beyond your short career, then you need to consider what has stood the test of time. And no one knows that better than Jesus.

When did Paul get smarter than Jesus?

I am really grateful for my training at one of the finest evangelical seminaries in the country, sitting under some of the best teachers and practitioners of my generation. Yet, had it not been for the abiding passion and influence of Dr. Howard Hendricks to focus on not only the words of Jesus, but the way He did ministry, I may have unwittingly given the relevancy of the life of Jesus a backseat to Paul.

The popular teaching of progressive revelation declares that the Apostle Paul had the latest and greatest revelation on theology for the church, and that even the teachings of Jesus must be interpreted in light of Paul's writings.

There is just one small problem with this. Jesus is God! As professor Dallas Willard had to remind us, Jesus is the smartest person who ever lived. He created life, knows the Kingdom of Heaven first hand, and has the truth you and I need for whatever we would be called to do in the Kingdom. I believe Paul would be embarrassed by this elevation of his writings over Jesus. Jesus' words are not commentary on the teaching of Paul! On the contrary, Paul's writings are the theological and practical application of the life and teaching of Jesus Christ.

We have wasted time wrangling over elders and deacons and whether women can speak in church instead of walking in the profound, mysterious teachings of our Lord. While arguing about church polity and the appropriate place of the sign gifts, we have let the prayer meeting die a slow death. Yet prayer, according to Jesus, was one of the marks of a faithful church.

In Luke 18:1-8 Jesus tells His followers a parable to show that at all times they ought to pray and not to lose heart, saying, *"In a certain city there was a judge who did not fear God and did not respect man. There was a widow in that city, and she kept coming to him, saying, 'Give me legal protection from my opponent.'*

For a while he was unwilling; but afterward he said to himself, 'Even though I do not fear God nor respect man, yet because this widow bothers me, I will give her legal protection, otherwise by continually coming she will wear me out.'"

And the Lord said, "Hear what the unrighteous judge said; now, will not God bring about justice for His elect who cry to Him day and night, and will He delay long over them? I tell you that He will bring about justice for them quickly. However, when the Son of Man comes, will He find faith on the earth?"

This parable of the persistent widow is given to encourage us to keep praying. A widow persistently pleads with a godless judge for justice and finally receives legal protection. The lesson is not that God is like the judge and must be "worn out" with our requests before He will act, but just the opposite! If this woman could squeeze justice out of this unrighteous judge, how much more can the elect expect God to hear their cry and act on their behalf?

Jesus ends the story with this test question: *When the Son of Man comes, will He find faith on earth?* The

According to Jesus, if we're not praying, we are not believing. In fact, you can't get much closer to the center of Jesus' will for your church than a prayer meeting.

connection is clear. Prayer is evidence of faith. According to Jesus, if we're not praying, we are not believing. In fact, you can't get much closer to the center of Jesus' will for your church than a prayer meeting. In Matthew 21:13 Jesus, quoting from Isaiah 56:7, said prayer would be the mark of His church: *My house shall be called a house of prayer for all nations.* It was in response to the teaching of Jesus that Paul called us to pray all the time, without ceasing.

Please don't misunderstand. I am not trying to diminish the importance of Paul. His explanation on what it means to be "in Christ," as just one example, is so necessary and profound to my walk that I will never fully plumb its depths. When Paul says we are in Christ, it is his commentary on the teaching of Jesus in John 15:4: *Abide in me and I in you.* It is my intention to give Jesus and His methodology for ministry, as well as His teachings, the place of prominence they deserve. After all, He is the Son of God. To assume that anything He did or said would become irrelevant is to be naïve at best and arrogant at worst.

Theologically, I understand the transitional nature of the Gospels. We are watching Jesus show men and women their inability to keep the Law and prepare them for the grace of the cross. For example, when Jesus tells the rich young ruler the one thing he lacks to inherit eternal life is to go and sell all his possessions, He is not telling us that we are saved by our works. He is pushing the religious self-righteousness of this young man to the limit that he might admit his inability to keep the Law and cry out for a savior.

Much of Jesus' teaching is relevant to the church and the Christian, particularly in the ways Jesus launched His ministry. This is what I would invite us to consider.

A.W. Tozer said about his generation, "Almost everything the church is doing today has been suggested by the world." My humble and persistent call is that we take our direction from the Leader, not from the fickle tastes and preferences of the culture.

> *A.W. Tozer said about his generation, "Almost everything the church is doing today has been suggested by the world."*

This book is not just for the professional. Whether you lead a small group study in your home or a Young Life club at your local high school, you want to see God at work in your ministry. You long to see lives changed by the Holy Spirit. You desire to see genuine conversions to the living Christ. Your aim is to see people set free from the lies of the enemy, to live in joy and fruitfulness. You intend to stay at it for the long haul. Jesus wants all this for us, as well. But we must do it His way.

What I discovered in Mark

As I studied the Gospel of Mark, seven practices or priorities of Jesus emerged. Startlingly, many of these are neglected in the modern pastor's job description. We are expected to do things that Jesus rarely, if ever, practiced.

At this writing, our church in Phoenix is going on nine years old. We started with a prayer meeting in our family room. Then we met in a high school cafeteria. We now serve a growing congregation in our own building. The elders of our church (which we call "shepherds" based on 1 Peter 5) found themselves overtaken with issues that did not look much like shepherding. What had begun as a simple and pure work of leading and discipling the congregation had turned into a "bored meeting" fraught with a never ending list of financial and facility issues. This was not what any of us had signed up for, but without a clear purpose and job description it's what elder meetings are destined to become: Does any of the following ring a bell? "The boy scouts want to use the building this week to do their annual squirrel dissection, but it lands on the same night that the over-eaters anonymous group hosts their bake sale, and you know what a hit that is?! Let's spend the next three hours writing up a policy the pastor can enforce."

There is a gravitational pull toward administration of lesser concerns if we do not intentionally stay with the call to make disciples.

We have discovered that we must regularly go back to the original recipe of disciple making to keep us on track as leaders. If we do not have a clear and purposeful agenda for our fellowship, the needs of men and the fickle appetites of the culture will set it for us.

As a pastor, I find that I must regularly retreat from the demands of church leadership to read and reflect on the Word and what Jesus wants me to be about. Which job description will Jesus bless, His or the one crafted by men? Why are we tired and burning out in tragic numbers? Is it because we are operating in the power of the flesh instead of the power of the Spirit?

You don't have to read very far into the Gospel of Mark before these seven priorities stand out in bold relief.

Calling

Preaching

Praying

Disciple-making

Spiritual warfare

Practicing the disciplines of the Spirit

Evangelism

Jesus does not set up a seminar and teach on these key ingredients to ministry in the Kingdom of God...He just starts doing it.

Introduction

Answering the call of our Creator is the ultimate "why" for living, the highest source of purpose in human existence.

(Os Guinness, The Call)

Chapter 1

Calling Brings Clarity and Confidence

I agree with Paul when it comes to calling, that each of us who loves Christ was chosen before the foundation of the world according to His grace (Eph. 1:4). And not only are we chosen unto salvation, but we are chosen with a purpose. Consider Ephesians 2:10: *For we are His workmanship, created in Christ Jesus for good works, which God prepared beforehand so that we would walk in them.*

Paul could not be clearer. We have a purpose! We are here in this time and place for a reason, to fulfill a calling of good works designed before the world began. Astounding, like most of the inheritance of grace. The great preoccupation of the believer is to know his or her calling and fulfill it, or so it should be. Sadly, many settle for fire insurance from hell and ushering or making coffee on Sundays once in a while. Is this what Christ prepared for you before the foundation of the world…to give yourself to asking, "Real or decaf?!"

We were given unique tools to fulfill our calling. 1 Corinthians 12 places great emphasis on God's design to give each individual believer a manifestation of the Spirit to be employed in the work of the Kingdom. You are called into the Body of Christ with a gifting to proclaim the Gospel and build up believers, whether that works itself out in quiet service behind the scenes or preaching the Word.

The point is that each of us has a calling as a follower of Jesus. As we will see in the opening chapters of Mark, calling is a major theme. And nowhere is the issue of calling more important than for those of us who sense the Lord is setting us apart for vocational ministry.

There is no question that one of the reasons for the large numbers of pastors abandoning their post is confusion about their call.

There is no question that one of the reasons for the large numbers of pastors abandoning their post is confusion about their call. Either they have lost sight of what they were called to be and do, or they responded to the call of a parent or mentor but not the calling of God.

As Eugene Peterson wrote in *The Unnecessary Pastor*, the culture sees our call "as paragons of goodness and niceness… custodians of the moral order…useful in a crisis." Wow! That will get you out of bed in the morning, won't it?!

Peterson goes on: "I am having the depressing experience of reading congregational descriptions of what churches want in a pastor. With hardly an exception they don't want pastors at all—they want managers of their religious company. They want a pastor they can follow so they won't have to bother with following Jesus anymore." *is your pastor this?*

Did you sign up to be a "religious manager?" I know I didn't. But that begs the question, "What did you sign up for?" It comes back to the issue of calling.

Mark opens his Gospel with a calling. John the Baptist was called in the womb (Luke 1) and sent as a preacher/messenger to prepare hungry hearts for the One who is coming. He dressed bizarrely, he ate the diet of the desert prophets, and he was completely un-intimidated by anyone as he preached this message of repentance. In his call to preach the truth, John took on the city fathers, the religious elite and Herod himself.

Where does such confidence come from? A great upbringing? Proper education? Strong genetics? I believe John was free to preach with boldness because his calling was so clear. Consider all the great men and women of God in the Scriptures. They had no power until they settled the issue of their calling. And the majority were not pastors, but kings, farmers, queens and fishermen.

Moses knew his calling early on, but lost sight of it as he began to trust in his credentials, his own strength, and his position in Egypt. Suddenly an Egyptian is dead by his hand and Moses must escape to the back side of the desert where he is broken and humbled. God comes to renew the call. Moses struggles with it, but once the issue of God's hand on his life is settled, strength and confidence return in large measure.

Joseph received a calling at an immature age, but would have to be broken and humbled before he could be a useful tool in the Lord's hand to literally save two nations! You see a similar pattern in David, Esther and Mary. Once the call is clarified, courage and conviction grow and the blessing of God follows.

My Calling

I was saved while attending Arizona State University in 1974, and immediately sensed a call from God to be set apart for some sort of service. I started a Bible study in my fraternity. I gave my testimony at Campus Crusade for Christ meetings and considered joining their staff. My girlfriend, whom I had led to Christ the same week I met Jesus, joined me in these activities but was reluctant to consider full-time ministry. We were married in

1976 after her graduation and began careers in sales and nursing. But my call would not relent, and God began to turn Margie's heart to see what He was doing with her new husband.

I'll never forget the day I finally gathered enough courage to tell my new bride of six months that she may have married a pastor instead of a financial planner! To my great relief, she quietly responded that the Lord had been showing her over the last couple months that this is what He was doing in my life, and that she was willing to follow me wherever He took us.

My sense of calling was confirmed by others in the Body of Christ as I served in a Young Life club, taught Sunday School, and accepted opportunities to speak and teach. I had a growing realization that nothing else would satisfy this growing hunger for His Word, to teach and preach it, to be used as a catalyst for growth in people's lives.

This seems to be the pattern, biblically and historically. The individual senses God's Spirit creating a hunger or drawing to preach or teach or serve vocationally, and begins to use their gifts in the local community. As fruit is born in their service, others confirm the gifting and sense that he or she is being set apart for vocational ministry. While I had the working of the

Spirit in my heart, I really needed the encouragement of friends and mentors to finally take the plunge.

Ministry is hard! It is humbling and confusing and puts an unusual strain on the family. If I were not able to rest in my calling, I know I would have left the pastorate by now.

> *Ministry is hard! It is humbling and confusing and puts an unusual strain on the family. If I were not able to rest in my calling, I know I would have left the pastorate by now.*

The pastor must be a theologian and a practitioner. He must keep deepening the well while tending to the needs of his congregation. He must know how to run a business meeting and have a word of hope for the woman dying of cancer in the hospital. He must mediate between a warring couple in his office and know how to hire the best staff and keep them happy. All this makes pastoral ministry both interesting and demanding. Without a clear sense of call as to why you entered the ministry in the first place, you will find yourself attempting to meet insatiable needs, growing more trite and shallow, and fighting a growing resentment toward the people and the God you claim to be serving.

Jesus' calling

Jesus has a very public calling to ministry in Mark 1 beginning with His baptism in the Jordan River and the affirmation of His Father: *You are my beloved Son, in You I am well-pleased.* His next forty days of testing and confirmation in the wilderness model for us the importance of setting apart those who are called.

The great mystery of the incarnation is that Jesus laid aside the power and privileges of deity and was conceived in the womb of Mary, and was born a genuine human child. He was vulnerable to the pain and indignities of real human life. He was hungry, tired, stubbed his toe, and felt the desire to punch a proud Pharisee in the mouth—all without sinning.

What I find most interesting is His dependence on the Holy Spirit. I think He was far more dependent on the leading and empowerment of the Holy Spirit than we are comfortable to accept. He really embraced becoming human, with all the limitations and challenges you and I face, so that His life could have real relevance to us. He models for us the life we are called to live, and practices the disciplines to walk in the Spirit.

At His baptism we see the Holy Spirit playing a major role.

8

In those days Jesus came from Nazareth in Galilee and was baptized by John in the Jordan. Immediately coming up out of the water, He saw the heavens opening, and the Spirit like a dove descending upon Him; and a voice came out of the heavens: *"You are My beloved Son, in You I am well-pleased."*

(Mark 1:9-11)

As Jesus comes up out of the water, the Spirit descends upon Him. In a moment, He is anointed, filled and equipped just as we are in our moment of conversion. Upon hearing the affirmation of the Father's love, Jesus is impelled or driven by the Spirit into the wilderness to pursue His calling.

Notice that both John and Jesus are taken to the wilderness for the confirmation and identification of their call. The world of men must be left behind so that these two remarkable men can be undistracted in their prayer and meditation on what the Father is doing in their life. The same was true for the Apostle Paul at his conversion and calling when he spent time in the Arabian Desert (Galatians 1:15-17).

How instructive for each of us. From the beginning of our salvation we must come under the influence and leading of the Spirit, which involves a "taking away" from our former world of friends and family in order to clarify who we are now and how we are to live our new lives. Each of the disciples will be personally called out by Jesus. Is this just interesting history? Or is Jesus showing us what He intends for each of us?

Your Calling

Have you just "volunteered to help" Jesus? The volunteer takes the initiative and reserves the right to stop whenever he wants. This is what drives us crazy in pastoral ministry! But when you are called, you have a whole different set of expectations and appreciation that go with the call. There is a personal connection—we wanted you! You are more willing to sacrifice out of gratitude for being called. You are eager to follow the lead of the one who has called you, by the very nature of the relationship.

How do you know if you have been called to full-time vocational service?

This is the mystery of faith, the mystery of your relationship with Jesus. It is like explaining when you know you are in love. You may struggle for the right words, but you know. So with the calling of Jesus to serve His church, you will know. You will be confirmed by others that God's hand is on your life, but first you must sense the call. You may have talents and gifts that people can see benefiting the church, but first you must sense His call on your life.

It is a call to serve, a call to forsake all other suitors, a call to come and die with Him. There can be no looking back, though there will be days of difficulty, confusion and heartache. It is a "fast."

It is a call to serve, a call to forsake all other suitors, a call to come and die with Him. There can be no looking back, though there will be days of difficulty, confusion and heartache. It is a "fast."

You will fast, or abstain, from the life of the average parishioner. You will never experience church as they do. You will never be as free to come and go as they are. You will never be seen by the community as they are. You have entered into a fast until the final feast. The Lord will not starve you to death, but will grow your soul fat on His Word and His blessing. But your life will always look and feel different from everyone else in the church. You must not fight this, but must accept it as part of the call.

The dangers of our call are real. No one has articulated them more clearly than Eugene Peterson in *Under the Unpredictable Plant*, page 3: "Our vocations are bounded on one side by consumer appetites, on the other by a marketing mind-set. Pastoral vocation is interpreted from the congregational side as the work of meeting people's religious needs on demand at the best possible price and from the clerical side as satisfying those same needs quickly and efficiently. These conditions quickly reduce the pastoral vocation to religious economics, pull it into relentless competitiveness, and deliver it into the hands of public relations and marketing experts."

As we keep our eyes on Jesus and His call we will find the clarity to not succumb to the centrifugal force of the demands around us. Remember the God; *who has saved us and called us with a holy calling, not according to our works, but according to His own purpose and grace which was granted us in Christ Jesus from all eternity!* (2 Timothy 1:9).

No two callings are the same

Don't be surprised if the call to serve Christ is not a straight line, but a winding journey of seeming detours, failures and restarts. I invite you to read through the Old Testament looking for the development of the call in the lives of men and women… no two are the same.

Abraham really has no background with this new God who has called him to do something no one from his family or hometown has any conception about…birth a nation! The fulfillment is long in coming, fraught with defeat and confusing experiences as well as grace and direction. The one constant is God.

Moses' call must "die" in the desert, where before encountering the burning bush, he "wastes" his best years tending sheep in obscurity before the burning bush. His lack of confidence is now understandable. Yet age and professional qualifications seem irrelevant to God, and the call persists.

David receives a call and a great confirming victory over Goliath, only to be sent alone into the desert by the sovereign hand and purpose of God. It will be years before the fulfillment of the call is realized. Yet David clings to God.

The point is clear. God's ways are not our ways. As different as David's experience is from Abraham's, so yours will be from mine. The common ground is our relationship with God, seeking Him and trusting Him, obeying Him and serving Him.

I love the attitude and passion of Paul in Philippians 3:14-15: *Not that I have already attained it or have already become perfect, but I press on so that I may lay hold of that for which also I **was laid hold of** by Christ Jesus...I press on toward the goal for the prize of the upward **call** of God in Christ Jesus.*

I have to keep coming back to the truth that ministry is not for me. It is for Him. I am not "making an impact." I am being faithful to my call. He does the ministry through me, with His tools. If I lay down His tools and take up the implements of men, I will build with wood, hay and straw. It may go up faster and the numbers may increase, but it will not stand the test of time.

I am the vine, you are the branches; he who abides (rests, remains, continues, stands) *in Me and I in him, he bears much fruit, for apart from **Me** you can do nothing.* (John 15:5)

I have tried ministry apart from Him, and it is exhausting. It breeds competition and comparison, it is addicted to the "take away," and it demands you hide your true self and perform. It feels more like driven than called. I want to live and serve worthy of my calling. I believe this is Jesus' desire for each of us, to *walk in a manner worthy of the calling with which you have been called* (Ephesians 4:1).

Our generation is seeing a wonderful influx of "second-halfers" into full-time vocational service. Men and women who have enjoyed careers in business or the professions now see that their skills and training match the church's need for wise administration and leadership. Like the disciples, they are "dropping their nets" and following the Lord into local church or para-church ministry. Our fellowship has benefited from many of these men and women, who bring tools to the table that our pastoral staff were never trained in.

My one word of caution is that the need does not justify the call. Although you have the skills from your career that would benefit the local church, be certain that it is the Lord and not the well-meaning desperation of your pastor that is drawing you to consider a vocational change. As I have said, the ministry is too hard and demanding to sustain on a hireling mentality. We do not need religious mercenaries to do the work of the church, but God-called men and women from all walks and stages of life, humbly responding to the invitation of the Spirit of God to serve.

We can always get more efficient than Jesus. He seems slow by our standards, choosing those we find less gifted or capable than others we would enlist for the cause. We have all read the Gospels and scratched our head at Jesus' choice of the twelve with their provincialism and prejudice getting in the way of their effectiveness and understanding of the Lord's mission.

This is the great temptation, to be smarter than Jesus about who and how He calls. I have had the humbling experience of pushing some sharp young man or woman of apparent great potential into leadership, only to be disappointed by their lack of character or commitment to carry the weight of the position. Better to wait and let that idea brew in your heart, than to jump ahead and launch a ministry with the wrong people. Believe me, I know!

If you are a lay leader in your church or ministry, I would encourage you to seek confirmation of your call and gifting. As we have said before, the need does not justify the call. Too many well-meaning believers are serving hard in ministries that

> *If you are a lay leader in your church or ministry, I would encourage you to seek confirmation of your call and gifting.*

are not their love or passion, but no one else would step up. Consequently, they are losing their energy and joy in ministry, and the work they were really called by God to do is being neglected. When we function in our area of call and gift, we sense the enabling and empowering of the Spirit. We have a lot more fun, more fruit produced, more life-change and more benefit to the fellowship.

Callings change and mature. The adventure is to keep growing and testing new waters to see if God is moving you into a new area of ministry and service. God's call usually involves some risk and change that will be uncomfortable. Can you find anything safe and familiar about Abraham and Sarah's call to wander in the desert? Moses and David had mid-life adjustments to what they understood to be their call, as did Paul.

My own experience has taken me from a large church senior pastor position with all the accompanying prestige and security to a mid-life call to plant a church from scratch in another state, uprooting three angry teenagers and a cat. Wrestling with God, excitement and anxiety all rolled into the process. The first couple years were both gratifying and excruciating. The call came with suffering for all of us in the Mason household, and there were dark nights with tears asking God if I had somehow stepped out of His will and blessing. I had regressed from overseeing a staff of fifty to setting up the chairs and restocking the bathrooms before preaching the sermon. What had sounded glorious and radical was back-breaking and anonymous. I was descending the career ladder while others of my age and station were solidifying their positions and planning for retirement.

I have come to see that God's call is as much about shaping my character as it is about productivity in His Kingdom. Just as He "wasted" Moses' forty years in the desert and David's ten years on the run as an outlaw, He may waste some of your best years to make you the man or woman He wants you to be. And when you look back, you see that those years were not wasted, after all.

Questions for Discussion

[handwritten: I love the Word and I want to show it to whoever will hear.]

1. How would you define your calling? How has it been confirmed for you? *[handwritten: Teaching — I want to share what I know of Him as I discover each new + fresh wonder —]*

2. What questions do you still need to resolve related to your gifting and calling? *[handwritten: I want to give back by discipling as I have been discipled.]*

3. As you consider the variety of calls in the Scriptures, which do you most relate to? For example: Abraham and Sara, Moses, Ruth, Esther, David and Daniel. *[handwritten: Whoever had the longest ~~that~~ wait before they were called to be fully used]*

4. Who have you encouraged in the pursuit of his or her calling? *[handwritten: Barbara M — encourager; BJ — prayer warrior; Jennifer Hasten Bowden — accountability; Nancy Kemp — preacher; missionary; Cheryl Nance — worship leader; Kathryn Dupont — preacher; Debbie G — preacher; Claudia Keith — hospitality]*

[handwritten margin: discipling, mentoring, and facilitating a Bible study and intro — how are they different? I know they are similar — how?]

Calling Brings Clarity and Confidence

I am certain that when I enter the pulpit to preach or stand at the lectern to read, it is not my word, but my tongue is the pen of a ready writer.

(Martin Luther)

Chapter 2
Preaching is Not Passé!

For since in the wisdom of God the world through its wisdom did not come to know God, God was well-pleased through the **foolishness of the message preached** *to save those who believe.* (1 Corinthians 1:21)

To the world, preaching has always appeared to be a foolish, arrogant method of communication. What could be less "politically correct" than one person standing before a congregation with a sense of the authority of God behind them?! As a speech communication major in college, I was taught that from a scientific perspective, preaching was an ineffective vehicle of communication. And for a time it appeared that the church was ready to scrap preaching as well. The idea of preaching, which sounded harsh and judgmental to modern ears, was being replaced by entertaining "talks" on a variety of subjects with a felt-need hook to the ear of the listener.

> *The idea of preaching, which sounded harsh and judgmental to modern ears, was being replaced by entertaining "talks" on a variety of subjects with a felt-need hook to the ear of the listener.*

However, like a person weary of always eating dessert, believers today are hungry again for the meat of the Word of God. The question is, will they be able to find a pulpit (now there's an outdated term!) that will feed them?

Jesus was the smartest, most insightful teacher who ever lived, and He was committed to preaching. From the beginning of the Gospel of Mark (1:4), preaching has a central role in the extension of the mission. *John the Baptist appeared in the wilderness* **preaching** *a baptism of repentance for the forgiveness of sins.*

The triune God determined that the best way to prepare the hearts of the people to receive Jesus was to send a preacher! And now when Jesus comes on the scene (Mark 1:14), He *came into Galilee, preaching the gospel of God.*

Later as His ministry develops (Mark 1:38), Jesus comes back from a time of prayer and solitude with the Father to lead the disciples to other nearby towns, *so that I may preach there also; for that is what I came for.* In Mark 3:14 Jesus chooses the twelve and summons them to Himself, that they might be with Him and so *that He could send them out to preach.* Jesus' final commission, as recorded in Mark 16:15, is to *go into all the world and preach the gospel to all creation.*

Let us not abandon or disparage this high and holy calling to preach the gospel! If it was good enough for the Son of Man and His disciples, it may still be good enough for us!

So the great apostle Paul, charging his protégé Timothy with the essence of his call in 2 Timothy 4:1-2, requires of him that he *preach the Word*! No other motivation is given other than that Timothy will give an account before Almighty God.

My friend and mentor, Bill Hull, put it succinctly in his book, *Complete Book of Discipleship*, page 181: "When we answer God's call to 'Come and be with Me,' we'll naturally connect the 'being with God' to 'going out to preach.' This is the way it works—for our good and for God's glory."

I confess that I love to preach. I love the sweet torture of coming into the office on Monday, knowing that Sunday is coming! I love to lay out the text, identify the main theme or idea, examine the details of definitions and grammar, reflect on the context, and then choose the application to my congregation. I love the challenge to stay fresh, to avoid clichés and Christianese, and to bring the theology of the text to life for an over-stimulated and over-informed yet Bible-illiterate generation.

To help our congregation get more out of the message, we have designed our small groups to study the passage I am preaching from *the week before*. My staff and I write a study guide for everyone in the group to get them into the text without answering all the questions. We want our people to have the joy of discovering the Holy Spirit speaking to them through the Word and enjoying the insights of their group members. As they come on Sunday morning, they are already familiar with the text and the issues, with the result that they get much more out of my sermon.

Expository Preaching

I am an expositor. That is, I typically take our people through a book of the Bible, preaching paragraph by paragraph. When we are in a lengthy book, like Isaiah or the life of David in 1 and 2 Samuel, I choose sections to make up a ten or twenty week series. Even when I am doing a topical series such as marriage or the vision of our church, I will choose one passage that speaks to the issue rather than a collection of verses.

There are four good reasons for expository preaching:

First, expository preaching gives the congregation a balanced diet of the whole Word of God. Over the course of a year, I choose books from both the Old and New Testament so that their love and confidence in the value of the entire Scripture is nurtured. Jesus' Bible was the Old Testament, and His teaching gave credibility to some of the more "fantastic" stories like Noah and Jonah. I think it is a safe bet that the average congregation is much less knowledgeable of the Bible than the preacher imagines.

If you teach a Bible study or lead a small group ministry, I invite you to set aside the latest new book and really teach your people the Word of God. The challenge is to teach it with creativity and relevance to their life and walk with Jesus. You don't need a seminary degree to be effective—just be a little further down the road than the ones you are teaching.

Second, expository preaching causes the preacher to raise the tough issues of life without the people feeling picked on. As they see you walking through the book, it is clear that this topic was raised by the text, not your personal knowledge of them. It also demands courage of the expositor to not avoid the tough calls to commitment and holiness that are salted throughout the Word.

3 Third, expository preaching gives glory to God! When we preach through the Word of God, we are declaring to the congregation that this entire book is God's revelation to us and more than able to equip us with all we need for serving Him and knowing Him. God is made great in the eyes of our people, for the Bible is a God-exalting text. In our culture of celebrity worship, the preacher or teacher is tempted to play to the crowd and the crowd is happy to oblige. The words

> *God is made great in the eyes of our people, for the Bible is a God-exalting text.*

of John the Baptist are instructive for me every Sunday: *I must decrease and He must increase.*

4 That leads to the fourth reason. I want our people to be more impressed with God than the preacher. Expository preaching is hard work. It demands my best hours in the day, my most creative thinking, and prayerful application. And the best test of my effectiveness is when our people come away from the service with awe and wonder in their heart for the God of the Bible—not me. It is easier in the short run to preach your favorite subjects, your humorous insights and catchy three steps to a better marriage or a good self-image. The problem is that you

run out of material. But with exposition, you will never exhaust the depths of the living Word of God.

Recently I read an article in our local paper about a group of Christians (by age and preferences what we would label the "emerging church") who were foregoing the traditional Sunday morning worship service for an evening meeting much like the small groups I just described in our own fellowship. While I completely understand and agree with the need for intimacy and sharing life together, or the preference for relationships over building programs and helping in the nursery, I am sensing a smugness that says we have discovered something better than preaching... conversation! No more arrogant authority figure telling us what to believe or think! We will discover the truth together in a dialogue versus the traditional monologue of preaching.

> *The Word of God could not be clearer that something happens in preaching that is unique from other forms of communication.*

Once again, we are getting smarter than Jesus! If only Jesus had had the insights of the small group movement, of

30

THE HEART of PREACHING (handwritten marginalia)

modern psychology and communication theory, He would have understood the ineffectiveness of preaching.

While, in the opinion of men, preaching may have lost its value in the modern setting, the Word of God could not be clearer that something happens in preaching that is unique from other forms of communication. Peter reminds those who preach to do so as *one who is speaking the utterances of God* (1 Peter 4:11). Paul tells the Galatians that *the gospel which was preached by me is not according to man* (Galatians 1:11).

When a man or woman stands before the people of God with the Word of God, called and gifted to preach, he or she must do so with all their heart and soul in obedience to this unique call. To do less is to make the congregation all the poorer and to risk the discipline of the One who called them. The people need to hear the Word of God preached! Preached with authority, humility, love and conviction, but preached nonetheless. The Holy Spirit does through preaching what He does nowhere else. Preaching is far different from sharing, counseling or even teaching. Preaching has a desperate quality to it—a dying man preaching to dying men. Preaching recognizes that this is the last day this person may venture into the church before giving up on God altogether. Preaching understands that the power of the Spirit of

Beautiful! I have heard this many times. It boils my bones and squeezes my heart (handwritten marginalia)

God and the Word of God delivered through the preacher of God can break a hard heart like nothing else. Preaching knows that for many listeners, this is the only time the Word of God will be opened before them. And the preacher must know that they are hungry for a word from the Lord—not from a man.

The uniqueness of preaching is that the authority of God imbues the moment with the Word of God to the benefit of the hearer unlike any other gift in the Body of Christ.

If Jesus were to appear today on earth to launch His mission, He would preach. He would preach on YouTube, Wall Street, Main Street and First Institutional, but He would preach. It is His chosen and Spirit-blessed vehicle for the gospel. As the great Puritan pastor Charles Bridges wrote in his classic work on the ministry: "It is not enough for us to speak the oracles of God. We must speak *as the oracle*." (p. 281, *The Christian Ministry*)

When Jesus describes the nature of the last days to the disciples in Mark 13, He warns them of frightening events that will grow in intensity: war, natural disasters, earthquakes, famines, and persecution of the faithful. These difficult days must be endured for one reason alone: *The gospel must first be **preached** to all the nations* (Mark 13:10).

Preaching is God's chosen and anointed method to reach the nations. Let us not shrink back from His call, but let us embrace the foolishness of preaching as further evidence that this is a supernatural work. It will never make sense to the wisdom of man, but it is the method Jesus chose for spreading His gospel for over two thousand years.

Any church or work of ministry that forsakes preaching as essential to the dissemination of the Word will fail to enjoy the full blessing of God (that is, if it continues to exist at all). Preaching is purifying, convicting, maturing and life giving when done in the Spirit of God through the Word of God.

Listening to Preaching Requires Preparation

Listening is a lost art, to be sure. Men and women from past generations listened to sermons that typically ran sixty to seventy-five minutes in length, and they recalled what was being preached! Listening to a sermon for the benefit of my soul is a learned skill. The disciple of Jesus will want to master listening, to be able to benefit from even a mediocre message and to take something away for his or her own ministry. Even a bad example is instructive. BECAUSE it is still His word through imperfection sent to us.

At a recent staff meeting, our team was bemoaning the number of regulars who do not bring a Bible into worship. The staff wondered if we were encouraging people to not bring their own Bible since we provided bibles at the back of the worship room and printed the scripture text in the bulletin, They may have a point.

When I listen to a sermon, I want to hear from God. I want God to speak through the human instrument before me using the Word of God and the preacher's own conviction and passion. If I don't have a Bible with me, I am at a great disadvantage in this quest. Moreover, if I don't have a pen and paper to record an insight or copy down a reference or illustration, I rarely remember by the time I reach home.

Listening is work. I need to be rested and reinforced with two cups of coffee (strong, black and hot). I prefer to sit near the front to avoid all the distractions of the people coming in late or getting up to call their bookie or relieve their tiny bladders. Listening to a sermon is not multi-tasking like watching TV while eating popcorn, drinking soda and reading the paper simultaneously. We need to come with expectation and a readiness to be confronted and comforted by the Word of God.

Preaching is spiritual warfare. As Jesus warned us in the parable of the soils in Mark 4:15; the devil wants to take away the Word that was sown in the hearts of the listener. *These are the ones who are beside the road where the word is sown; and when they hear, immediately Satan comes and takes away the word which has been sown in them.* We need to come prayerfully to the sermon, asking God to deliver us from temptation and distraction and to open our ears that we might hear Him. This is why it is typically best to have the preaching follow the worship time so that hopefully our souls have been opened up by worship and the grace of God so that we can receive His truth.

Children Need Preaching Too

One of the great losses for our children is to keep them from the worship service and preaching because we believe they will be bored and disruptive. I confess this is the tradition in our fellowship, and it makes me increasingly uncomfortable. I have heard many testimonies of elementary age children responding to the preaching of the Word, moved by the Holy Spirit, with results that lasted into adulthood.

Let's not get smarter than Jesus regarding our children! It seems the disciples had the same mindset in Mark 10:13-16. They were correcting the children and parents for attempting to be touched and blessed by the Savior. Adults only. With anger and frustration Jesus corrected them, saying: *Permit the children to come to Me; do not hinder them; for the Kingdom of God belongs to such as these.*

Most children and youth ministries today are heavy on entertaining. Consequently, the young person has a diminished sense of the fear of God. Preaching with passion impresses the developing conscience with what is to be feared and avoided as well as what is to be pursued.

And what about the child whom God has called to a preaching ministry? Where will she find her inspiration? Where will she see her parents eyes fill with tears and shout "amen" in heartfelt agreement? Where will she sense the holy hush of conviction as the Spirit breaks proud hearts with the sword of the Word? Our

> *Our children need training more than entertaining. Let's train them to sit under the preaching of the Word of God.*

children need training more than entertaining. Let's train them to sit under the preaching of the Word of God.

Imagine if the tide turned in our nation and all the tax privileges were taken away from churches and ministers of the Gospel. We were now being asked to pay our fair share of property tax and income tax on the offering, and all housing allowances were removed. Many fellowships would have to put their facility up for sale, or cut back staffing to the bare bones. At this point, what would the church continue to do? Things would get much simpler. We would look a lot more like the first century church. We would have to get back to the basics…like preaching.

As Charles Wesley proved with his meetings in the warehouses, and George Whitefield effectively preached in the open pasture, we don't need stage lights and microphones and multi-million dollar buildings to preach the Word. We just need a gifted and called preacher and an occasion to meet. Just like Jesus did.

Preach the Word!

Preaching is Not Passé!

[handwritten note in margin: Is this Directed towards preachers or all Christians?]

Questions for Discussion

1. What has been your experience with preaching? Has it been important to your own growth in grace, or is it diminishing in value? Why is that?

   [handwritten: Dynamic - exciting - eye, ear and heart opening]

2. What has made preaching most effective for you?
   As a listener. *[handwritten: Always going back to the Holiness of God - the source]*
   ~~As a preacher.~~ *[handwritten: Get grounding in every-day application the balance of the]*

3. How do you feel about women preachers? If preaching is a gift, can you find where the gifts in the New Testament are gender specific? Consider these women: Miriam, in Exodus 15:20; Deborah in Judges 4:4; Anna in Luke 2:36, Acts 2:17; 21:9, and 1 Corinthians 11:5. Are they not proclaiming the Word of God to men and women?

   [handwritten: Most Dynamic! Debbie & Antkya D — mission]

4. What is the difference between teaching and preaching, as a gift and as you have experienced it?

   [handwritten: preachers - tell you the truth flat out - no "niceties"]

Preaching is Not Passé!

Prayerlessness is my declaration of
independence from God.
(Daniel Henderson, *Fresh Encounters*)

Chapter 3
Praying is The Work of the Ministry

There was a time when this would be the first chapter I would skip in a book. Not that I didn't believe in prayer or its importance, but prayer had become something boring and guilt producing. It was the last meeting I would want to attend, and I was a paid professional!

The subject of prayer had become like my neighbor harping on recycling or the latest study on why I shouldn't drink so much coffee. I knew they were right, but it seemed to be more about "ought to's" and taking the fun out of life rather than putting it back in. Compared to the three hours Martin Luther devoted every morning, I knew I didn't pray enough, so why even try? And I wrestled with the concept of a God who had to be coerced into hearing my requests by labored, long-winded bouts of intercession.

And I wrestled with the concept of a God who had to be coerced into hearing my requests by labored, long-winded bouts of intercession.

If you find yourself having the same emotional mindset to prayer, I want to lure you to read on with the promise of longer life and a better golf score. (Oh come on, it works for the televangelist!)

To my great surprise and by the grace of God, my attitude toward prayer has done a complete turn-around, and I would like to share how it happened. But first let's make the case for the importance of prayer.

I believe the greatest indictment on our generation of pastors and Christian leaders is the loss of confidence in calling our people to regular times of corporate prayer. The prayer meeting has gone the way of the organ and hymnals; relics of the past. The consequence is a church and leadership that have put their confidence on the wisdom of men, not the promises of God. God is too slow for our taste. Our culture wants something to happen and happen now! It is easier to find the right talent, the right music or program, and give the people what they think they need rather than wait on God for what they really need…Him!

Bill Hull, one of the leading voices on disciple-making, puts it like this: "The church has been doing the right thing—working to build the cause of Christ—in the wrong way—depending on competence rather than a prayerful life of dependence on God." (p. 295, *The Complete Book on Discipleship)*

Prayer was clearly a top priority of Jesus, but what does He know? He must have had to pray more, right, because He lacked all the resources that we enjoy in ministry. On the contrary, from the beginning of His ministry when he seeks solitude and prayer for forty days, He is modeling for us the true source of our power and passion.

The first day of His public ministry is a full one. As Mark records in chapter 1, this particular Sabbath day begins in the synagogue with preaching and teaching and ends in Peter's house healing and casting out demons with the *whole city gathered at the door* (v. 33).

The next morning as the disciples look for Him, Mark tells us that Jesus had gone to a secluded place to pray. It appears that He needed this time with the Father to gain clarity about His purpose, since He was being inundated with people's needs. As Jesus clearly demonstrated, the need does not justify the call.

Let us go somewhere else to the towns nearby, so that I may preach there also; for that is what I came for. (Mark 1:38)

It was in prayer that Jesus stayed centered on the main thing, to preach the gospel. Without this time alone with the Father, He would be tempted to stay at Peter's house and meet the myriad of needs waiting at the door. And make no mistake, He wanted to do that. His heart is full of compassion for the suffering of these people. Just like you and me. As pastors or Christian leaders, we must follow Jesus in a life of prayer or we will find ourselves trying to serve the never-ending demand of human need and suffering. We'll come back to this in the chapter on spiritual disciplines.

When the disciples asked why they had failed to cast out a demon from a boy in Mark 9, Jesus' answer to their question, "Why?" was clear and to the point: *This kind cannot come out by anything but prayer* (Mark 9:29).

What did He mean? No human power can combat the spiritual hold of demonic possession or oppression. No human authority can break this grip. Only the power of God in the authority of Jesus Christ can deliver from the forces of darkness.

Prayer is a demonstration of my dependence on God. Conversely, prayerlessness is a demonstration of my confidence in myself, or a loss of confidence in God—common occupational hazards of ministry.

More on this in the chapter on spiritual warfare, but the point is that prayer is the work of the ministry. Prayer is a demonstration of my dependence on God. Conversely, prayerlessness is a demonstration of my confidence in myself, or a loss of confidence in God—common occupational hazards of ministry.

House of Prayer? Really?

We spend far more time, money and effort on our music ministry than our prayer ministry. The result is what you'd expect: marvelously talented and gifted musicians and singers turning our congregations into an audience instead of the army of God. Don't misunderstand, I love great worship music! Music is a real gift of God to the church and to the believer in his personal and corporate worship. But our priorities could not be more upside down if music takes precedence over prayer in the church.

And He began to teach and say to them, "Is it not written, 'MY HOUSE SHALL BE CALLED A HOUSE OF PRAYER FOR ALL THE NATIONS.' But you have made it a ROBBERS' DEN." (Mark 11:17)

Jesus declared that His house should be called a house of prayer. Our churches can be called many things...house of preaching, house of children's programs, and house of music. But when were we ever called a house of prayer?

Prayer humbles me. Prayer reminds me of my inadequacy to produce spiritual fruit. In prayer I hear Jesus say, "Without me you can do nothing."

Jesus wants us to come boldly and pray for mountains to move! (Mark 11:23) He wants us to move mountains of unbelief, mountains of suffering and pain, mountains of injustice and wickedness. The vision of the church, humanly speaking, is beyond her resources, but entirely possible in the strength and enabling work of God. And this comes by prayer, the work of the ministry.

As Christian leaders, we must call our churches, small groups, and ministry teams to pray. We must set the pace. We must model it. Only God will know. It will be the great test of our integrity and the difference between merely performing and bearing real fruit.

Our church in Phoenix was birthed in a prayer meeting in our family room. My wife, Margie, wisely challenged me to start with a prayer meeting instead of a Bible study. "Everyone will come to a Bible study," she said, "but a prayer meeting will surface the people you really want to plant a church."

Once Desert View Bible Church was launched, we committed to a monthly prayer meeting that would be a part of the church as long as she was under my leadership. Our lay leadership took the call to pray even further by establishing a prayer team of about forty adults who pray every week for an hour over the needs of the people. The result is that prayer requests are brought before the Father daily for thirty days. We have been amazed as God has answered our prayers on a consistent basis for healing, jobs, salvation and restored relationships.

Prayer can become a dry discipline if we lose the vision for what it really is…co-laboring with God to see His will be done and advance His kingdom purposes. The more we pray, the more we think to pray. Prayer affects our entire personality, shaping, strengthening, and conforming us more into the image and ways of Christ.

Clearly, the privilege of prayer was one of the greatest gifts of the cross, opening the way to the holy heart of God without shame or fear of condemnation. Let us not neglect this great opportunity and privilege unique to the people of God.

I challenge you as a pastor or Christian leader to make prayer a greater priority in your own life and the lives of those you lead. Personally, I pray best in community. Allow and welcome the gifts of others to help you to maintain this commitment to be a praying leader, a praying church.

At Desert View we have made prayer a part of our worship service, often spontaneously as we sense the Spirit leading us. We invite people to let us know they need prayer that morning, and those worshiping around them lay their hands on them as I pray from the platform. We send our teams off with prayer as they go to do mission work or take an important role in our fellowship.

As I write these words, our country is in the greatest financial crisis since the Great Depression. Millions of dollars have vanished overnight in lost home equity and investments. Government solutions only seem to make the problems worse, increasing debt while rewarding those who made poor choices at the expense of those who were frugal. The greatest suffering is felt among those with the least financial margin: single moms, the elderly, and children of the poor.

Yet, where is the call to pray and seek the mercy and intervention of God? Not one political leader has called a news conference to invite the nation to pray. We have become either too proud or too stupid to know where to turn. It is time for the church of Jesus Christ to step up, to let our voice be heard in heaven. It is time to call the church to her knees to intercede on behalf of the nation.

Like Nehemiah, we must be driven to cry out to God about this great nation's financial and moral devastation. We must confess our sins, repent, and turn to God with all our heart. It is the church's hour in America. May she hear her call to pray! I long for God to renew me and my church, to bring conviction of sin and a hunger to share Christ with our community. Prayer is the way. It was Jesus' way. May it be the mark of our lives and that of our churches.

> *I long for God to renew me and my church, to bring conviction of sin and a hunger to share Christ with our community. Prayer is the way. It was Jesus' way.*

Our city of Phoenix is blessed with a real man of prayer in Pastor Juan Ramos of Love International, a church that was birthed out of a prayer meeting in his home. I have worshipped with him and his congregation on Tuesday night, where over a thousand people come to worship and pray every week. His invitation to his people has not changed over the last twenty years. He asks them to come and let him ***pray for them.*** The love and connection shared by pastor and congregation is a direct result of the weekly time of being prayed over by their spiritual father.

The Gospel of Mark is salted with examples of Jesus praying over people. Why have we neglected this privilege? Perhaps we have become discouraged by prayers not being answered. I have certainly felt the tension of praying for others about issues that God had not yet resolved in my own life. Nothing exposes our humanity like praying for others. Our theology of the grace of God is central to prayer, or it will die on the vine. If we are performing or earning the right for God to move, we will finally collapse under the weight of unmet expectations. Grace reminds me that all things are a gift from God, that my praying is that of a dependent child before a loving father.

Prayer is difficult because it is so important. It is the source of real power, real life change in me and my congregation. I should expect opposition from within and without.

Why are we not captured by the idea of a prayer meeting? Perhaps it goes back to a childhood experience of being dragged to a prayer meeting. Endless. Boring. The same people praying. Prayers that seemed more about them looking spiritual than really calling down the power of God. Spending more time telling the prayer request than actually praying. You promising yourself that once you were old enough to choose, a prayer meeting would be the last place you'd be found on Wednesday night!

I have certainly been guilty of leading a bad prayer meeting. Whether it was because I was ill prepared, or let certain well-meaning souls dominate the time, I know what it is like to leave thinking the only reason I would ever come back is because I have to! I am still learning what it means to lead an effective prayer meeting. We experiment with music and worship, planned and unplanned elements, directive and spontaneous praying to involve more people and create a place for God to move and speak. Sometimes we sense His presence among us and sometimes it is dry, but we stay at it. We have committed to be a praying church with a prayer meeting, regardless of current taste or trends. We want to become a house of prayer as Jesus desires.

The prayer meeting deserves our best! Our leaders must attend and show that it is their priority. The music (if you have it) and worship must be quality, Spirit-filled and appropriate to the moment. Those who lead the meeting must have prayed in preparation. I have had the uncomfortable experience of leading the people in prayer and feeling like I needed to re-introduce myself to God...it had been a long week! Certainly we operate under His grace and longsuffering with our humanity, but our level of preparation will communicate the value of the meeting to our people.

When I consider the strong invitations from Jesus to pray, I must make it a priority for myself and my church. While I cannot fully comprehend the power and protection that comes through prayer, I believe it. The keys of the kingdom of God seem to be accessed by prayer. To do ministry without a foundation of prayer is to bang on the door but not know how to open it. Prayer is listening for the voice of the Savior, waiting on Him and trusting Him to lead and guide us.

C.S. Lewis, in his *Christian Reflections,* pages 142ff, struggled with petitionary prayer, calling it "a problem without an answer." Passages like Mark 11:23-24 left him wondering what he was doing wrong when he didn't see the result Jesus seems to promise: *Truly I say to you, whoever says to this mountain, 'Be taken up and cast into the sea,' and does not doubt in his heart, but believes that what he says is going to happen, it will be granted him. Therefore I say to you, all things for which you pray and ask, believe that you have received them, and they will be granted you.*

Lewis observes that the experience of Great Britain during the bombing raids of World War II did not square with this promise of moving mountains. Certainly British believers prayed with faith, and yet the Nazis rained devastation on their cities. They prayed for peace and no peace came. As Lewis puts it in his own unparalleled style: "It is the faintest suspicion of excess in the advertisement that is disquieting." (p. 151)

Many Christians have been silenced in their prayer life by these same questions. Their experience just doesn't seem to match with what Jesus promises, so they must be doing something wrong. Either they are not spiritual enough, or they think are not praying in the right way. In any case, it quenches one's desire to pray. And this is a real problem when you are the leader of the prayer meeting!

My own wrestling with this problem has brought me to this conclusion: God is doing far more than I can

My own wrestling with this problem has brought me to this conclusion: God is doing far more than I can see or appreciate from my small and limited perspective.

see or appreciate from my small and limited perspective. He is moving mountains that I am not fully aware of or could even understand if He tried to explain it all to me. Like a child asking his daddy to let him drive the family car, the answer must be no for now, but with the understanding that a day is coming when he will be able to drive. It is beyond the child's capacity to understand all the reasons, so he must simply trust his daddy.

I would rather keep praying and bringing Jesus' own promises before Him with childlike faith than to stop praying out of frustration because the mountains don't seem to move. Gethsemane reminds me that there are times I must be content with *Not my will but Thine be done.*

Let's not get smarter than Jesus on prayer, complicating it with questions that cannot be fully answered this side of heaven. Let's just pray and take Him at His word and leave the results with Him.

Brothers and sisters, let us pray!

Praying is The Work of the Ministry

Questions for Discussion

1. What is your greatest hindrance to prayer; theologically or practically?

2. What has been your experience with corporate prayer meetings? What do you think about reviving them in the local church? What benefits? What obstacles?

3. As you think about Biblical models or teaching on prayer, which are most motivating for you?

4. What are you doing with the people in your area of ministry to teach them to pray?

Praying is The Work of the Ministry

The crisis at the heart of the church is a crisis of product. What kind of person does the church produce?

(Bill Hull, *The Disciple-making Pastor*)

Chapter 4
Disciple Making and the Power of One

My father-in-law had a ranch in southern Utah where my family vacationed every summer for over twenty-five years. Homer was a fighter pilot and major general in the Air Force by career but a farmer/rancher at heart. Now in retirement, he filled his beloved Pine Valley with all kinds of animals for his grandchildren's delight. It was here on the ranch that I saw the power of *bonding* or *imprinting*, which is highly instructive in relation to Christians and following Jesus.

One summer, a mother hen hatched the cutest collection of chicks we had ever seen. My wife and daughters were especially attached to them, and watched them begin to explore their world. At the same time, a female duck was nurturing some young ducklings down at the creek, just a few yards from the barn. Things got interesting when the family of chicks came near the creek and the ducks.

Somehow, one of the chicks bonded with the mother duck and her ducklings as her family! To our horror, the little chick followed the ducks to the creek bank, into the water, and proceeded to sink! Our daughters ran to save her, took her to the house, and used the hair dryer to fluff her out. But when we put her with her chicken family, she headed right back to the creek to seek out the ducks. Again she tried to swim in the creek and began to sink, was saved by my girls, and returned to her chicken family. We finally had to confine her in the barn for her own safety.

That little chick had bonded with the ducks and saw herself as a duck. The strongest image right after this little chick hatched was the mother duck, and there was no changing her orientation.

In the same way, I have observed that newly-born Christians bond to the example of the Christian life lived in front of them, and it shapes their vision of the Christian life, for good or for ill. For example, I was birthed into the faith in college by a fraternity brother who took me immediately to a Campus Crusade for Christ

By contrast, many people come to faith in their home or a church where the image they bond to is one of passivity.

meeting. There I met other new converts, was warmly welcomed into the fellowship, and challenged to start growing and to share my faith…tomorrow! I was indoctrinated in the "win-build-send" model of the Christian life. My initial bonding with these people continues to shape how I view the life of a disciple of Christ.

By contrast, many people come to faith in their home or a church where the image they bond to is one of passivity. The model before them is this: come to meetings, give of their finances and then get on with their "real life." In this model, it is not the average but the extraordinary Christian who actively shares his faith, ministers to the poor, or meets with others in a small group to study the Word and grow.

After almost thirty years of church ministry, I have seen that this initial bonding or imprinting of a passive life of believing but not following is not easily overcome! How we start the Christian life is how we will envision it for most of our life, unless God intervenes.

In the Gospel of Mark, we see Jesus imprinting his new recruits with the right vision. Jesus doesn't enroll them in a degree program or a classroom of any kind. It is not an invitation to help administrate his ministry. He simply says, "Follow Me, and I will make you fishers of men."

Amazing! What a powerful invitation. It is personal and it is missional! Jesus is not asking them to believe, but to follow. He is going somewhere. Obviously, they would have to believe something about Him to take Him up on His invitation, but the call is to join Him in going somewhere. It is an adventure.

By contrast, we call people to only believe. Do you believe you are a sinner and Jesus died for you on the cross? Yes? Just pray this prayer and you're "in." That sounds more like the finish line than the starting gate. How we communicate the gospel, and how we model it, is how it will be lived out by our hearers. Jesus called you and me as leaders in His church to make disciples (Matthew 28:19-20). Paul urged the believers to become "living sacrifices" (Romans 12:1-2) who could be made "complete in Christ" (Colossians 1:28).

Let us stop asking for converts and make a call to follow Jesus. Following assumes we believe who He is and what He said and did, or we would not follow Him.

If I told you I believed Lance Armstrong is one of the greatest cyclists of all time, I would not necessarily be telling you that I rode a bike. I could believe this truth about Armstrong without being into cycling, myself. But if I told you I was a follower of Lance Armstrong, or a student of his, or that he was my mentor, you would rightly assume that I rode a racing bike and attempted to compete like Lance. I would be more than just a fan...I would be a disciple of the sport.

Many people believe Jesus is their Savior, believe He is the Son of God, and believe He is coming back. Sadly, they are not followers, but fans. The church should be making followers, not fans of the Living Christ!

As Bill Hull makes clear in his many books on the topic, disciple making is not pursued because it is slow work without the benefit of quick results. It is not a church growth strategy, it is not the felt need of most inquirers to your church, and sadly it is not the experience of most church leaders. And you cannot reproduce what you have not experienced.

I am making the call for pastors and church leaders to get back to Jesus' model to make disciples. This model is to commit to a small group of men or women to walk after Jesus with love, honesty and accountability. To practice the disciplines of the Spirit, like prayer and Bible memorization and solitude in

Professionalism has killed disciple making in the church. As the clerical, or professional class came into the forefront of the local church, the laity became spectators.

community with a close-knit fellowship of your own. To factor a multiplication mentality into your group so that what they experience with you they will eventually replicate with their own group.

Professionalism has killed disciple making in the church. As the clerical, or professional class came into the forefront of the local church, the laity became spectators. The new convert was simply expected to come to the services, give their money, and manage their sin. The clergy would pray for the sick, study and preach the Word, lead people to Christ, and provide all the religious services of weddings and funerals, etc.

Please don't misunderstand me. I believe that God's plan is for the local church to be led by a called and gifted group of pastors, teachers and evangelists to establish and build up the fellowship.

And He gave some as apostles, and some as prophets, and some as evangelists, and some as pastors and teachers, for the equipping of the saints for the work of service, to the building up of the body of Christ; until we all attain to the unity of the faith, and of the knowledge of the Son of God, to a mature man, to the measure of the stature which belongs to the fullness of Christ.

As a result, we are no longer to be children, tossed here and there by waves and carried about by every wind of doctrine, by the trickery of men, by craftiness in deceitful scheming; but speaking the truth in love, we are to grow up in all aspects into Him who is the head, even Christ, from whom the whole body,

(James 1:16).

(Rom 12:4)

being fitted and held together by what every joint supplies, according to the proper working of each individual part, causes the growth of the body for the building up of itself in love. (Ephesians 4:11-16) *(Col 2:19)*

ø   But over the centuries we have adopted the classroom model of the Greeks in place of the disciple-making model of Jesus, resulting in an elite class of professionals who have all the knowledge and training to do ministry to and for the members of the congregation. I am simply calling for us to get back to the disciple-making model of the Savior. The local church does not need more classes. It needs more mentors and disciple makers to come alongside the hungry young converts and lead them in the disciplines of following Jesus.

Accountability Required

First Jesus calls the various individuals who will make up the twelve to follow Him. He has only a short time to build the foundation of a ministry that will continue on when He is physically absent. Let us make Jesus' first priority ours, as well. After all, this was His last instruction to His followers before the ascension: *Go and make disciples of all nations...teaching*

them to observe (keep, obey, guard) all that I commanded you
(Matthew 28:19).

My own journey as a follower of Christ is marked by the men who loved me and invested in me, personally and regularly. They discipled me. Our times together took on a variety of venues and purposes, but the common denominator was their commitment to help me grow in Christ and to be my friend. Consequently, I have always met with a small group of men to grow together in our "followership" of Christ. I need the discipline, and they need the experience of being in a discipling environment.

The key difference between a discipling group and other small group experiences is the intentional commitment to learn skills and habits that are transferable and user friendly. Let me share from my own experience.

I launch a group by praying and asking God who I should invite. When I hear from God, I extend that person a personal invitation. I can say without hesitation that we do too many shotgun appeals from the platform and too little personal and prayerful inviting to join a group or ministry. Many may jump at the chance to be in my small group, but only the Lord knows if they are ready to grow and commit. I want the men Jesus chooses. Left to my own devices, I will choose men too much like me, sharing my interests and sense of humor. The best groups have diversity of age, background and gifting.

The group usually consists of four to six men including myself. While there are times when a man needs one-on-one spiritual counseling and discipling, I find the best dynamic is a small group of men (or women, depending on your gender). The variety of gifts and perspectives provides a rich mix to the group that is beyond the leader's capacity.

You may find yourself in a home fellowship of men and women like our Community Groups that meet weekly studying the text to be preached the following Sunday. These groups are critical to building friendships, ministering to one another, and growing in the Word together. It may be that the men or women you disciple come from this group. The point is that there is a level of honesty and accountability that happens in the discipling cell of four to six people of the same gender that just does not happen in a mixed home fellowship of ten or fifteen. We need both kinds of groups in our lives.

In whatever ministry you find yourself, whether it is the worship band or loving the toddlers, there are adults around you hungry to be discipled. Use your natural connection of relationships to see who the Lord would lead you to invite. While our church has used the "organizational" approach of mass sign-ups and cold starts with people who have never met for our Community Groups, the goals and commitment of a discipleship group require a more prayerful and relational foundation.

In whatever ministry you find yourself, whether it is the worship band or loving the toddlers, there are adults around you hungry to be discipled.

At the first meeting I lay out the commitments involved and give everyone a gracious "out" if this is more than they are ready for. The reality is that if you have prayed about the group members and invited them, they are hungry for this kind of opportunity and will arrange their schedules to accommodate. God's people want to be challenged and want to grow in their relationship with Christ. The church has too often failed these hungry-hearted souls by asking them to just come, enjoy the show, and chip in a few bucks.

The commitment looks something like this:

- Meet every week for a year, then re-evaluate.
- Be on time and always call if you know you will be absent.

- Come prepared with your notes on the study and your verse memorized.

- Be praying for the men in the group during the week.

- Start thinking and praying about the men you'll invite to a group you will start.

I really make the point about multiplication that first meeting. This is not a dead-end group. This is not another notebook to put on the shelf. This is a training group in which you will have opportunity to lead and practice the skills you will bring to your group.

The first months are devoted to learning to study the Word and feed ourselves with a view to be able to teach others. I take the men through the basics of Bible study methods:

Observation   What does it say?

Interpretation What does it mean?

Application   What does it mean to me?

As we practice laying these three grids over the text, it gradually becomes second nature to approach the scripture with these questions. We crawl before we walk, so we take a verse at a time, then a paragraph, and then a chapter. The rewards of learning to study and unlock the Bible for oneself are life-long and give the individual the confidence he needs in the Word to disciple others. Without this skill, they are doomed to be forever dependent on fill-in-the-blank booklets and re-digested truths of others. That's not good enough. My goal is to produce thoughtful followers of Jesus who find the Word of God bearing fruit in their own life so they have a harvest to share with those they lead.

When we planted Desert View Bible Church, I took the twelve men who made up our shepherd team and put them in three groups of four men whom I met with every week for breakfast. We memorized verses basic to our walk with Christ and relevant to the mission of our new church. We shared our lives and began to love and trust one another more deeply. The vision of multiplication was made clear, as well, so that they would be looking and praying for future leaders for the movement.

Along with the time in the study, there needs to be occasion to do life together. Sharing meals with spouses, playing with the kids, going on a retreat or taking in a movie are all part of growing in love and appreciation for one another.

The Force of the One

In ministry, the great temptation is to spend time with the neediest people or those who demand the most attention. The consequence of this is that the people who can make a real contribution are often the most neglected. We recruit them, give them a job, then move on to the "squeaky wheel." Not surprisingly, many of these highly committed individuals leave the local church for para-church ministries or some place where they can receive the more personalized mentoring and discipling they are hungry for.

In the ministry of Jesus, His priority is to invest time with the twelve. The needs around Jesus are vast and without end, but they do not drive His agenda. While He gives Himself to heal and teach the masses, He is regularly pulling back to be with the men He called unto Himself. When He is gone, it is not the masses who will carry on the work but the men He has invested in.

In college I had a poster on my wall that read something like this: "The force of one committed person is equal to 99 who have only an interest."

In college I had a poster on my wall that read something like this: "The force of one committed person is equal to 99 who have only an interest." Even as an unbeliever, that statement captured my imagination and earned a place in my dorm room. I knew in my gut that this was true, whether in sports or academics or business. Now I know it is true in the kingdom of God.

The goal of my ministry is to find, disciple and launch the One. I understand that he will be hidden among the masses and will not necessarily demand my attention. Like the disciples Jesus chose, he may not have religious qualifications to set him apart. We will have to seek the One out or he might surface as we are doing the work of the church. But he is the One who will make a difference in the church and in the kingdom. He is the Christ-centered, committed One and he is typically dissatisfied by what the church offers him.

We tend to want one-size-fits-all in the church. Everybody take class 100, advance to 200, then 300, and now you have got it. Now you are discipled in what it means to follow Christ and ready to make disciples yourself! Get on our conveyor belt of adult formation and at the end of the ride you will "be discipled." Most people are compliant and want to play ball with us so they can become part of the church. But the highly committed One is bored by this hand-holding approach to the greatest adventure of their life. He needs more.

The One needs to be mentored by someone willing to come alongside and learn what God is currently doing in his life. He is already praying and talking to his unsaved friends about Christ and wants help on how to reach them. The One wants to understand how to study the Word for himself. He wants to spend a day away with you to learn how to hear God and to find deliverance from the things that plague him.

The One wrestles with questions: should I go to seminary? Or can God use me right here and now to make a difference in my world? The One wants to invest in the kingdom. He wants his life to matter for Jesus. He doesn't want to waste it.

These highly committed people need and deserve the time with and discipling by our best people, but this is not what usually happens in the church. Leaders and pastors are besieged with pastoral needs and providing weekly services that leave little time for "hanging out" with the One, let alone prayerfully looking for and identifying who he is.

The heartbeat of the One is summed up by Jesus in Mark 8:34-38: *And He summoned the crowd with His disciples* (note that this is a word for everyone, not just the inner circle) *and said to them*: *"If anyone wishes to come after Me* (not converts but followers), *He must deny himself, and take up his cross and*

78

follow Me. The One understands this and expects that is what it will take to follow the Savior. Just like learning a new language or getting in shape to run a 10K, the One is not surprised that he will have to say "no" to some things in order to say "yes" to Jesus and being His disciple. The One is looking for other like-minded disciples who can encourage him on this journey.

For whoever wishes to save his life will lose it, but whoever loses his life for My sake and the gospel's will save it. The One sees the futility the world is offering him. He sees the destructive power of his own appetite and pride and is looking for a way to break free of their addictive hold and give himself without reservation to something big and glorious like the service of King Jesus.

It appears that Jesus has been extending this invitation for over two thousand years, but the church has diluted its potency by milder interpretations or relegated it to the professional elite but not the masses. Yet I have found that the One is looking for just this sort of challenge. Let's get out of the way so he can hear Jesus call him out.

Who is the One? A young teenage girl longing for something more than a world focused on her bust size. Or a forty-something executive finally tuning in to his heart's cry, "Is this all there is?"

Maybe it's a burnt-out pastor willing to give Jesus and His way one more try. What will the Church prescribe? Take this class? Read this book? Get some counseling? Or will there be a like-minded and like-wounded discipler who has been praying for just such a One to come across his path.

When I stand before Jesus, He will not be holding our attendance records in his hand, nor the budget, nor even the doctrinal statement, important as all these things are. I believe He will show me His disciples, people in whom I invested my life and skills, the men who are discipling others. Jesus called disciples to make disciples. He wants to make them through His church. Let's obey the Lord of the harvest and make disciples.

Questions for Discussion

1. Considering the story of the chick that thought she was a duck, what was your early bonding experience related to discipleship and growing in your walk? Who were your models? What has stuck with you over the years, for good or for ill?

2. What have been your most satisfying experiences in disciple-making? What are the challenges you face in thinking about a commitment to make disciples?

3. How do you respond to the idea of "the One"?

4. What skills and habits are you passing on? Which ones would you like to sharpen?

Disciple Making and the Power of One

The fundamental biblical opposition is not between flesh and Spirit, creature and Creator, but between the Creator of the flesh and its destroyer, between God and the devil, Christ and Satan, the Holy Spirit and the Unholy.

(Philip S. Watson)

Chapter 5
Spiritual Warfare is a Path to Freedom

Sitting with me in my office are my friend Dr. Neil Anderson and a woman who was a part of my youth ministry back in the day. Since graduating from high school, she found herself involved with drugs and drug users, finally leaving the state of Arizona with her pusher and husband for Michigan. Now she is back home with three kids and a raging addiction to meth, begging for God to set her free. She has a genuine relationship with Jesus and has prayed many days and nights to break the hold of the drug. She has tried twelve-step programs and found she could not stay clean. She has left her abusive husband and wants to keep her children, but knows all is lost if she can't shake her craving for meth. We are her last hope.

Neil is a world-renowned author, seminary professor and founder of Freedom in Christ Ministries. He has seen many people like my friend, and worse, set free from the demonic hold of drugs and a horrid past.

As we lead her through the steps to reclaim her true identity in Christ, we ask her to read a renunciation of Satan and his lies and to declare her security in Jesus. She tries to read, but the letters blur and run together. Her breath becomes labored. Fists clenched, her face contorts in a painful grimace. "I can't breathe," she cried, and bolts from the room. I chase after her, assuring her that there is plenty of oxygen in the room and that this is a spiritual attack to keep her from renouncing the devil and his lies in her life. Because she trusts me, she comes back into the room. Neil calms her down, explains that Satan has no authority over any of us in the room, that Jesus is here and in charge, and that we should continue.

Slowly, achingly she declares her identity in Christ and renounces the work of the devil in her life and addiction. As she continues to make declarations about who the Bible proclaims her to be and asks Jesus to break the demonic grip on her life, her whole countenance changes! Her hands relax, a smile I had not seen for years comes over her face and she declares with joy and conviction, "I am free!" I know I will never forget the transformation I witness that afternoon.

That day the chains were broken in my friend's life. She continued to battle her flesh and the old life style, and even had a couple of setbacks. But she always came back to Jesus and grew stronger. Today the Lord has given her a new husband, a church family and real hope for the future.

That day was also an education for me. We cannot be passive about the spiritual battle. Please don't misunderstand me. This was no exorcism, no naming demons and inviting a confrontation. It was a simple process of repenting of past sins, acknowledging the demonic and spiritual holds that come with habitual sin, and seeking to break those chains in the authority of Christ.

Since that meeting in my office I have had many opportunities to lead people to a new level of freedom in their walk with Christ. It has become clear that a spiritual battle is at the

It has become clear that a spiritual battle is at the root of many of our emotional and spiritual problems

root of many of our emotional and spiritual problems, and that a passive approach to the enemy of our souls will not break the chains that hold so many Christians in bondage.

Why are we surprised? Because we think we are smarter than Jesus when it comes to demonic activity in our modern age. After all those uneducated first century New Testament writers had to use demons to explain what we, in our enlightenment, know as epilepsy or Tourette Syndrome, right? We know better.

The problem with this explanation is that it implies that Jesus and the Bible are suspect. If all the Biblical accounts of demonic activity, are false or understated, we are deceived and misled. So what else has Jesus been dishonest about?

On the other hand, if Jesus and the New Testament writers intended for us to be aware and equipped to deal with this malevolent reality, we'd better pay attention. Anyone who is paying attention at all when he or she reads the Bible, and particularly the Gospels, will be confronted with the reality of the spiritual battle.

Genesis introduces a crafty, powerful and dangerous being whose mission is to misrepresent God to us and lead us into destruction: *Now the serpent was more crafty than any beast of the field which the LORD God had made. And he said to the woman, "Indeed, has God said, 'You shall not eat from any tree of the garden'?"* (Genesis 3:1).

Job, perhaps the oldest book in the Bible, takes us behind the curtain to see the activity of Satan and the access he has to the presence of God.

Now there was a day when the sons of God came to present themselves before the LORD, and Satan also came among them. The LORD said to Satan, "From where do you come?" Then

Satan answered the LORD and said, "From roaming about on the earth and walking around on it"

The LORD said to Satan, "Have you considered My servant Job? For there is no one like him on the earth, a blameless and upright man, fearing God and turning away from evil."

Then Satan answered the LORD, "Does Job fear God for nothing? Have You not made a hedge about him and his house and all that he has, on every side? You have blessed the work of his hands, and his possessions have increased in the land. But put forth Your hand now and touch all that he has; he will surely curse You to Your face."

Then the LORD said to Satan, "Behold, all that he has is in your power, only do not put forth your hand on him." So Satan departed from the presence of the LORD. (Job 1:6-12)

To this day the evil one is not smoldering in hell, but brazenly intruded into the holy throne room of the Almighty, accusing and slyly asking permission to tempt and deceive the saints.

Daniel is visited by an angel who, while coming to Daniel's aid, was delayed by a cosmic battle with demonic powers over the city (Dan. 10).

Paul and Peter don't seem to buy the "mythical character" explanation. In their epistles, both warn us of our spiritual enemy and tell us to equip ourselves for battle (Ephesians 6:10-18 and 1 Peter 5:8-9).

John's Revelation is a complete unmasking of the cosmic conflict, with the forces of the Lamb marshaled in victory against the dragon and the beast. How can we miss the message of the Scriptures shouting with one voice from Genesis to Revelation... We are at war!

Spiritual warfare in Mark's gospel

As we come to the greatest event in human history, the incarnation of God in the person of Jesus Christ, the forces of darkness are threatened and stirred up like a hornet's nest. In fact, the first order of business for the Messiah after His baptism is to give the devil every opportunity to tempt or dissuade Him from His mission.

No sooner has Jesus successfully rebuffed the devil in the wilderness and begun preaching the Gospel than we find Him confronted by a man with an unclean spirit in the synagogue.

The demon knows who Jesus is, and knows its fate is in His hands.

Just then there was a man in their synagogue with an unclean spirit; and he cried out, saying, "What business do we have with each other, Jesus of Nazareth? Have You come to destroy us? I know who You are—the Holy One of God!" (Mark 1:23-24)

In Mark 1:32 Jesus finds Himself in the home of Simon Peter where people are bringing *those who were ill and those who were demon-possessed.* Evidently Jesus was not confused about the difference between disease and demons.

Another sobering example is found in Mark 5:1-20. A man from the Gentile region of the Gerasenes is filled with many unclean spirits. Jesus commands the demonic beings to come out of the man and go into a herd of swine, which they promptly drive over a cliff. The surrounding business community, more concerned with their future commodity trading than the reality that God is in their midst, beg Jesus to leave them.

Another dramatic encounter is portrayed in Mark 9:14-29, where the disciples find themselves unable to help the son of a desperate man. A demonic spirit has made the boy mute, regularly slamming him to the ground where he writhes, foaming at the mouth. When the father asked the disciples to help, they were not able. Jesus rebukes his men with words that haunt the church and her leaders today: *O unbelieving generation, how long shall I be with you? How long shall I put up with you?*

In our unbelief we have tried to solve spiritual problems with human wisdom. What are we to

> *Is it not clear that where Jesus is at work the forces of darkness in people's lives will be stirred up?*

make of all these demonic encounters? What message is the Holy Spirit conveying to us? Is it not clear that where Jesus is at work the forces of darkness in people's lives will be stirred up? Is it not clear that even believers can be attacked and harassed by Satan and his ilk, as seen in Jesus' warning to Peter during the Last Supper? *Simon, Simon, behold, Satan has demanded permission to sift you like wheat; but I have prayed for you, that your faith may not fail; and you, when once you have turned again, strengthen your brothers.* (Luke 22:31-32)

One of the ministries of our shepherding team is to pray for the sick. The congregation knows that they have only to ask and we will be glad to ask for the Lord to heal. On one occasion, a woman came for prayer who clearly loved Christ and was active serving Him in our congregation and her neighborhood. She had been plagued for years by Lupus-like symptoms, was taking several medications and still finding little relief.

As is our custom, we asked her if she had been involved in anything of the occult or sin patterns that would give the dark spirits a hold on her life. She mentioned that in her last job there were several lesbian women who resented her faith and had even told her they had put a curse on her. Based on our young but growing understanding of the spiritual battle, we asked the woman to renounce the curse with us in prayer and that Jesus would break any hold on her life from that experience with those women.

A day or two later I received a phone call from the woman's husband. She felt so good after meeting with us that she took none of her medications and had a peaceful night's sleep. She went to her doctor the next day where he confirmed the absence of symptoms and took her off the medications. Please don't misunderstand. I am convinced of the need for medication and psychological counseling. My concern is that we have put all our hope in chemistry and neglected the reality of the spiritual battle.

The Battle Ground

When Paul tells us that he takes every thought captive to the obedience of Christ (2 Corinthians 10:5), he is addressing the battle for the mind. There is no biblical evidence that the devil can read our minds. He is not God.

The greatest need of the hour is for Christians to know who they are in Christ.

But he is like a radio transmission broadcasting disparaging and blasphemous ideas and seeing who will tune in. For the majority of people we have helped in our ministry, these accusations are the place of defeat. They are Christians who have believed lies about who they are, either from guilt and shame about their past sins or from bad theology based on works and performance.

As Neil Anderson has proclaimed in all his books and messages, the greatest need of the hour is for Christians to know who they are in Christ. We need to be trained to act on the truth that we are beloved children of God, saints who sin, that all has been forgiven, and that God is for us. No one has done a better job of summarizing these truths than Dr. Neil T. Anderson in his *Steps to Freedom in Christ.* We buy these booklets by the case.

We have been too passive about the spiritual battle. Whether out of fear or ignorance, we have been swatting at the wrong target to find relief from spiritual and emotional oppression. Please don't misunderstand! I am a strong advocate of biblical Christian counseling and know that not all our problems have a demonic or spiritual dynamic. But it is my experience that, to our own defeat, we have erred on the practical and human wisdom side of the equation.

As human beings, we are not compartmentalized into body, soul and spirit. We are deeply and mysteriously integrated beings, so that emotional and spiritual problems have mental and physical manifestations. One touches and impacts the other. I am simply calling for this recognition and a greater awareness of the bondage in which Christians can find themselves due to demonic oppression and satanic lies that they have come to own.

As we minister to a generation of greater brokenness and deeper experiences of sin, we should not be surprised to see a greater prevalence of demonic attachments. Through habitual practices of illicit sexual activity, pornography and drug abuse, the forces of darkness are inadvertently invited to have a place in the person's mind and heart. Conversion enables a person to cleanse his life of these attachments. But then in a process of repentance and renunciation, he must address the demons work of evil in his life.

The battle ground is the mind, where the enemy seeks to defeat us in our walk by implanting lies about who we are and who God is. The Liar's strategy is to keep us from the riches of our inheritance in Christ and to remind us of our past failures and abuse so that we wallow in shame, guilt and bitterness. A combination of meditating on the truths of Scripture and making peace with our past is essential to breaking the hold of these lies.

If Jesus and Peter were targets for the evil one's attacks, we should not be surprised that Christians committed to Christ and engaged in kingdom work are in his malevolent sights. This should be a matter of prayer and regular conversation, to keep our thinking straight and our perspective clear about where the real fight is located. As Paul reminds us in Ephesians 6:12, the battle may look like a human problem but the source of the conflict lies in the realm of the invisible: *For our struggle is not against flesh and blood, but against the rulers, against the powers, against the world forces of this darkness, against the spiritual forces of wickedness in the heavenly places.*

I can say without hesitation that the most painful experiences and trials in our family have occurred during this season of church planting. When Margie and I answered the call to come back to my home town of Phoenix and plant a church, we were naïve and unprepared for the chaos the enemy of our souls would stir up to try and discourage us. The family and relational strife reached such a crescendo that I found myself on my knees asking God how I had stepped out of His will. Surely I must have done something wrong to be in this much pain and frustration! In my hunger for direction, I fell upon 2 Corinthians and Paul's own experience of rejection and misunderstanding with the very church he had planted and established in Christ. Evidently this was par for the course with church-planting! Oops, I must have missed the fine print in the manual...

Time, the Word, and some godly mentors helped me to see what was going on. The forces of darkness wanted to destroy this new work of God by defeating the pastor and his family. While we still bear the scars of this battle and the attacks continue from a variety of fronts, we know better how to pray and where to put the blame. The trials were not evidence that we were out of God's will, but just the opposite. Every genuine work of God will experience spiritual resistance from the enemy. Jesus did, and He assured us that we could expect the same:

I will build my church; and the gates of Hades will not overpower it. (Matthew 16:18)

Strategic Prayer in Warfare

Remember Jesus' word of explanation as to why the disciples could not drive the demonic spirit from the young man: *This kind cannot come out by anything but prayer* (Mark 9:29).

No Christian leader or minister of the Gospel should attempt to do the work of the kingdom without a covering of prayer. If Jesus is showing us what we can expect as we preach the Gospel to a godless generation, then the protection and authority of prayer must surround our ministry.

No Christian leader or minister of the Gospel should attempt to do the work of the kingdom without a covering of prayer.

As I mentioned in a previous chapter, at Desert View we have about forty adults who pray every week for the specific requests of the congregation and for the staff and leadership of our church. Every week! What a sense of security that gives me as I preach the Word and lead the body in the work of the kingdom. Whatever victory we are experiencing in counseling and making disciples, I give credit to these faithful warriors who bring the needs of our fellowship before the Lord every day.

In conclusion, we are faced with a choice. Either Mark's gospel is a dated piece of mythology when it comes to demonic spirits, or Jesus is giving us a vivid picture of what we are up against as we seek to make disciples. Through the Word and my own experience in local church ministry, I have come to see that spiritual warfare is real and must be addressed if we are ever to see people set free in Christ.

How sobering to read Jesus' words in Mark 8:33 to Peter, who has just attempted to dissuade Jesus from the cross: *Get behind Me, Satan, for you are not setting your mind on God's interests, but man's.* Jesus knew who he was dealing with!

Our intentions may be honorable, but when we substitute for scripture what makes sense to men, we may be siding with the prince of darkness, not the Prince of Peace.

Let's not be smarter than Jesus when it comes to spiritual warfare.

Questions for Discussion

1. What is your background when it comes to this teaching? On a scale of 1 to 10 (with 1 representing complete passivity about the subject and 10 looking for demons behind every bush) where would you place yourself? (7)

   NO BACKGROUND ON THIS TEACH-
   ING, BUT I BELIEVE WHAT JESUS
   WARNS OF.

2. What does it mean to you to understand who you are in Christ? How is our identity in Christ related to spiritual warfare?

   HE IS IN ME AND I IN
   HIM BECAUSE HE CHOSE ME AND
   I ACCEPTED HIS GRACE. HE "INDWELLS"
   ME AND THEREFORE (Rom. 8:29-31)

3. Where do you currently feel spiritual attack in your life and ministry? How do you discern this? *(Rom. 8:38-39)*

   ISOLATION from fellow CHRISTIANS
   MAKES ME EASY PREY for DOUBTS
   AND NEGATIVE SELF IMAGE.

4. What authority do we have as believers when it comes to our enemy? Ephesians 6 is a classic passage in this *OF faith* regard. What is the warning of Jude 1:9 in this regard?

   WE HAVE THE AUTHORITY of
   JESUS CHRIST, SON of GOD.
   WE DO NOT HAVE THE AUTHORITY
   AS IS POINTED OUT IN (JUDE 1:9)

Spiritual Warfare is a Path to Freedom

To undertake the disciplines was to take our activities—our lives—seriously and to suppose that the following of Christ was at least as big a challenge as playing the violin or jogging.

(Dallas Willard, *The Spirit of the Disciplines*)

Chapter 6
Spiritual Disciplines, the Pathway to Renewal

One of my favorite story plot lines is the time machine. Whether going back in time like *A Connecticut Yankee in King Arthur's Court* or bringing historical figures to the modern age, the changes in the way we do life and how we would be viewed and measured by our forefathers make for entertaining books and movies.

What would Jesus and the disciples make of our frenzied and constantly-available existence in the twenty first century. Instead of overturning a table of money changers, I wonder if Jesus would reach into my briefcase and throw away my electronic devices. As one writer observed, through cell phones, pagers and PDAs, we live in a constant state of preoccupation. We can't be fully engaged in the moment because we are distracted by an email that just popped up on our iphone. We are texting and twittering to an invisible audience whose greatest fear is to be disconnected from this inane (and insane) flood of trivial information.

If ever there were a harassed and exhausted generation, it is ours! On a recent trip to India, I had the rich privilege of getting to know young Indian believers working in the growing phone center and tech industry. Sadly, they shared stories of ten and twelve hour work days, six days a week; a schedule that leaves little time for family and church involvement. Yes, they were enjoying a higher standard of living than their parents, but at what cost? They were poorer in relationships and the simple pleasures of just spending time together.

Pastors and church leaders attempt to superimpose a grid of discipleship over this harassed life style only to find there is no real transformation. As my friend Bill Hull has observed, when preaching meets culture, culture wins! Preaching in and of itself is not enough to see lives changed. There must be an intentional plan to lead our people to rearrange their lives around the practices of Jesus. These are the spiritual disciplines.

From the opening verses of Mark, we are introduced to two men who have set themselves apart to be faithful to their call. John the Baptist chooses to live in the desert, away from the pull of the culture and well-meaning friends and family, so that he might call out a fellowship of people looking for God. Everything about him—his dress and his diet—shout that he is not of this world, which is exactly what makes him so attractive to people who want God. They don't want to be entertained or have their egos stroked by false religious profiteers. They want God, and they sense this holy man has God's hand on his life.

Jesus makes a dramatic start to His public ministry by retreating into the desert wilderness for forty days. Made strong by the time of deprivation in which His spirit was undistracted and attuned to the heart of the Father, Jesus meets his nemesis and defeats him at every temptation. Full of the Holy Spirit, He now is ready to preach the gospel of God. The response to His message and His power is immediate! Crowds form outside the door of every house he stays in. The needs are overwhelming and never ending, and the word of His fame is spreading like wildfire. His next move is startlingly powerful in its simplicity and contrast to what is happening around Him: *In the early morning, while it was still dark, Jesus got up, left the house, and went away to a secluded place, and was praying there* (Mark 1:35).

Really, Jesus? You mean you were not "prayed up" from the forty days in the desert just a few days earlier? Are you not aware that momentum is building, that you should strike while the iron is hot and build as large a following as you can? As the disciples declare in exasperation, "Everyone is looking for you!"

Isn't that always the issue for us in ministry? Everyone is looking for us! The phone is ringing, the in-box is full, the calendar is filling up, the recruiting list has holes, and the fundraising is already too small for the need! And the dirty little secret of those of us in ministry is—we like it! We like to be needed, to be important, to be the key person, to feel busy!

We've really outsmarted Jesus on this one, haven't we?! With all our technology and availability and communication ability, we've just about run ourselves into the ground.

We desperately need to learn and practice the disciplines of the Spirit that Jesus models for us in the opening verses of Mark. Not to impress God or others, let alone to earn some spiritual benefit from God, but simply that we might survive and thrive.

As you read the Gospels, you never get the idea that Jesus is in a hurry. He is doing the most important work that any human ever undertook, yet without haste. The demands on his person are certainly as great as ours, if not more so. The human pain and suffering around Him is immense. How easy it would be to cave in to the tyranny of the urgent and lose sight of the larger goal. The key was His commitment to

As you read the Gospels, you never get the idea that Jesus is in a hurry. He is doing the most important work that any human ever undertook, yet without haste.

retreat, to be alone with the Father. He wants us to get this, to do what He did.

Rest for Your Souls

The groundbreaking book for me on this whole idea of the disciplines was Richard Foster's *Celebration of Discipline.* I was a youth pastor at the time, and could not wait to take my junior and senior high students away for a retreat to practice these ancient pathways to spiritual renewal. To the surprise of many of the adults, the students loved the opportunity to be silent and alone in a beautiful setting, to memorize and mediate on a portion of scripture and learn the art of journaling.

It was with the students that I saw the power of practicing the disciplines in community, where there is encouragement and accountability to stay with it. This lesson has stayed with me to this day. In fact, many people give up too soon on these habits because they are attempting to do it alone. Jesus' model of the small group as a place to practice these habits of the spirit is our best hope. We need one another.

Busyness is the scourge of our culture. When we play the trump card of being busy, no one (not even our guilty conscience) can challenge us. We profess that we are busy when in truth we are wasting some of our best time on activities and people that will not produce much fruit for the kingdom. The people we are leading want to know, as they should, that we are spending time with God. And giving ourselves to the things which they are unwilling or unable to give themselves. We cannot lead anyone where we ourselves have not been.

Busyness is the scourge of our culture. When we play the trump card of being busy, no one (not even our guilty conscience) can challenge us.

Three disciplines have been the most powerful and restorative for me—two that you might expect and one that may surprise you.

The Discipline of Solitude

The first call is for the pastor and Christian leader to seek solitude on a regular basis to be in the presence of God. Alone in the quiet with the Word, we pour out our heart to a loving heavenly Father. We rest in the arms of a Savior who was tempted and tested just as we are. He knows. He gets it. Like David, we hold nothing back, but bring all that grieves us, burdens us and discourages us to Jesus.

Solitude is the first discipline, for all the others flow out of it. If we cannot really be alone and still before God, we will never experience the power of prayer. We will never hear the cry of our own soul. We will never enter His rest that He promised us in Matthew 11:28: *Come to Me, all who are weary and heavy-laden, and I will give you rest.*

I would not trust any Christian leader who doesn't practice solitude. Being alone with God is the mother of all the other disciplines.

We are the most harried, most pre-occupied generation of humans the planet has ever seen. Sadly, we may have to forcefully pry the blackberries from one another's clenched fists as we seek mutual accountability to experience real solitude, but it must be done.

I would not trust any Christian leader who doesn't practice solitude. Being alone with God is the mother of all the other disciplines. If we have not become comfortable with our own thoughts and the beating of our own heart, we will never really be comfortable listening to God. God will not shout to us over the music, the TV, the texting, or even "the ministry." Jesus had to pull away regularly in His ministry to be refreshed, to commune with the Father and keep clear on the purpose of His short time on earth.

When I fail to get away and seek out times of solitude, my emotional and spiritual tank begins to run dry. I lose intimacy with God and depth in my thinking if I stay too long on the week-to-week, Sunday-to-Sunday treadmill.

All the men used of God in the scriptures discovered the gift of being alone with God, either by choice or by circumstance. Consider Enoch, Moses, Joseph and David as men who found greater depth and trust with God when meditating on Him and His Word in the field, the desert or the jail.

We are at a great disadvantage from our spiritual parents. They traveled in the quiet of walking or riding a horse. They worked in the quiet of an orchard or farm. Their days began with the sunrise and ended with sundown. More than that, as a regular part of their life and worship, they were surrounded by the glory of creation.

You and I are burdened by the modern city, cars, busses, phones and television. It takes a concerted effort and real planning to seek out a place of uninterrupted quiet. But it must be done!

My favorite places are where I can walk in a forest or desert path undisturbed. Listening to sounds of the birds and stopping to study the intricacies of a flower remind me that God is all around me. I see His beauty and His character in what He has made. To appreciate the glory of God in creation is to bring Him pleasure and to have a fuller appreciation of who He is. I love to go to zoos and botanical gardens to worship Him! His creative genius and artistic brilliance are on display in the vast variety of creatures and vegetation.

Living in the beautiful Sonoran desert of Arizona has provided me rich lessons on the nature of God. Most people come expecting the place to look like the Sahara with miles of rolling dunes of nondescript sand. On the contrary, our desert sits at about two thousand feet above sea level and is lush with trees, cacti and shrubs of all species. What at first glance looks dangerous and harsh, upon closer analysis reveals a softness and intricacy of design that is mind blowing. Just like God.

A cursory reading of Genesis may leave one believing that God is severe and judgmental, dispensing curses, floods and dispersions of people. But a more thoughtful investigation reveals a God with a heart to bless, forgive and restore. Solitude, alone with Him and what He has made, invites us to see more deeply what the busy eye will miss.

It is in these times of solitude that I read the classics of the Christian life in short, digestible portions. I find a passage and let it simmer in my mind and heart so that the depth of what God is saying may have a chance to resonate in me. I pray out loud. I whisper to God. I shout and dance and fall on my face. Frequently I weep before Him, releasing the flood of emotion that every leader carries from broken dreams and unmet expectations.

These experiences with God cannot happen in a fifteen minute devotional before work, or praying in the car. Every believer needs to learn how to do this, but it will not happen until leaders begin to live it and model it. Those whom we disciple must be invited to participate in these times to learn how, as it does not come naturally at first.

Most people will be initially uncomfortable with the quiet, or will find their minds filling with anxious thoughts. Men might battle a preoccupation with lust. Women may struggle with all that is not getting done while they are "goofing off with Jesus." But over time and with some practice, solitude will become the sweetest of times with God, mini retreats that you will look forward to as you schedule them in your calendar.

The Discipline of Memorizing Scripture

We have really gotten smarter than Jesus on this one. Why memorize the Word when we can pull it up on our laptop, iphone or e-reader? When we view the Bible simply as another piece of information for a message or Bible study, we have really become clueless about how the Word of God "works."

We are biblically malnourished and underfed in the midst of plenty because we have not learned how to feed our heart and mind on God's truth. Memorization is like chewing and digesting. In our pseudo spiritual culture, we take a bite, taste it, and go on to the next meal. We are told *about* the food, its ingredients, who prepared it, etc. But we are not really eating—we are just tasting. Consequently, instead of being strong in the Lord we are weak. The Word is our meat, the food for our soul. But we have forgotten how to eat!

I will never forget a conference I attended in which Dr. Dallas Willard, author and professor of philosophy at USC, was speaking. Willard is God's voice to call us back to the disciplines, to understand them and make them a part of our lives. On this occasion, someone asked him which of the disciplines or habits of his walk with Jesus had the greatest impact on his transformation. Without hesitation, he said, "Scripture memory had the greatest impact on my walk with God."

Jesus fought the temptation and manipulation of the evil one in the wilderness with Scripture He had memorized. And it is safe to assume that the disciples were also memorizing the Word, as they did not have the luxury of leather-bound personal Bibles to carry around.

In Mark 4 Jesus explains how life works in the kingdom, the foundational parable of

> *Without hesitation, he said, "Scripture memory had the greatest impact on my walk with God."*

the four soils (or the parable of the sower). The constant in the story is the seed, the Word of God. The variable is the kind of soil or heart the Word is planted in. A soft, receptive heart will hear the Word, assimilate it and bear fruit. The Word is key to fruitfulness. We are nourished by the Word as we think and chew and finally believe what it says and do it.

The enemies of memorization are also given in the parable. The first heart is hardened by busyness and self, and the Word is snatched away before it can penetrate. The second heart has failed to take the Word in deeply through memorization and meditation, so the resulting shallow roots render the Word fruitless. The third heart is full of activities in competition with memorizing and meditating on the Word, and so the fruit is choked out.

The Bible is not magic. Putting it under my pillow at night does not release its power in my life. Most Christians have a short morning devotional a couple times a week, maybe a Bible study as part of their home fellowship, then a sermon two or three times a month. On the surface this looks like a regular "feeding" in the Word, but that's the problem—it's on the surface! In reality, it is too shallow an application to cause any real growth in one's life.

What are we growing, grass or trees? Grass can thrive on a sprinkling a few times a week, but a tree needs a deep soaking at least once a week that reaches the depths of the roots. In our desert environment, if you plant a tree in the lawn where you are just sprinkling, you will tease the roots of the tree to come to the surface. The result is a tree with shallow roots that will topple in a summer monsoon storm.

Psalm 1:3 reminds us we are trees, not grass, and that we require a deep soaking in the Word to be fruitful: *He will be like a tree firmly planted by streams of water, which yields its fruit in its season. And its leaf does not wither, and in whatever he does, he prospers.*

Memorization is God's method to deeply soak us in the Word. It is most effective in community with other believers, encouraging each other to do the work and being accountable to come with our memorized verses ready to share. We all have many regrets in life, including how we used our time and what we filled our mind and heart with. But I can guarantee you that no one ever regretted memorizing the Word of God! I have regretted some services I planned, some sermons I preached, and some programs we have launched. But I have never apologized for challenging our people to memorize the Word, and I cannot challenge my people to do what I myself am unwilling or too lazy to do.

The discipline of serving the poor

This is the one I thought might surprise you. I'll never forget the first time I went with my good friend Billy

Thrall, a pastor and missionary to the poor in Phoenix, to do the chapel service at the medium-security jail for adolescents who had committed a felony. After passing through the metal detector on the first floor, we step into an elevator which takes us to the underground passageway to the jail pods. No attendant, no screen telling us what floor we are passing, as we go down. The doors open and we walk the cinderblock and linoleum hall, turning here and there, until we reach another elevator. We announce to a faceless speaker/receiver that we want to go to the third floor for a chapel service. The doors open to the floor and a guard takes us to the chapel room, with chairs, some Bibles, a TV and VCR. After a few minutes, the guards usher in a group of inmates, all in their prison garb, ranging in age from 15 to 18. While they may have looked pretty tough on the mean streets of Phoenix, in here they just look like someone's son.

I have 50 minutes to worship with them and preach the gospel, and I am having the time of my life.

I brought no manuscript of a past message, just my Bible. On the drive to the jail, Billy and I prayed and decided who would do the preaching today and I took the call. I have almost nothing in common with these mostly Hispanic and African-American teenage felons, except that I understand fear and hope and I know the God who loves them and wants to reach them. I actually feel privileged to be in this jail at this moment. I feel as close to the center of God's will for my life as I ever have while preaching in the 'burbs.

Our current church property lies on the growing suburban fringe of the metro-Phoenix community. I can go through my week and rarely be disturbed by the needs of the poor with the exception of someone coming in for gas or food coupons. The danger of this suburban ministry is that we lose touch with the very people with whom Jesus spent the majority of His time. Jesus came to "preach the gospel to the poor" (Luke 4:18). Consequently, I choose to minister to and with the poor for the sake of my own soul and to be in touch with my Lord.

Consequently, I choose to minister to and with the poor for the sake of my own soul and to be in touch with my Lord.

Ministry among the poor is a spiritual discipline that has blessed me far beyond whatever I have brought to them. As long as I stay in my own ghetto of middle class problems and needs, I am tempted to rely on my own training and experience. After all, I know these people and their problems and I know how to help them. Unfortunately, I can also become embittered by their fickle consumer mentality toward the church and find myself in competition with the bigger ministry down the street. Attitudes that shrink my heart.

By contrast, nobody is in competition to serve the poor. There are always more needs than any one person or ministry can meet. With the poor I am always out of my element, feeling very white and privileged and forced to look at the promises of God differently for people with very different life experiences and challenges. The poor help me see that all I really have to give them is Christ in me (which is also true in the 'burbs but easier to forget).

A study of the economics and sociology of first century Judea will make it clear that Jesus was preaching to the poor. By poor, I mean people who are living day to day, hand to mouth. They do not have savings or farms, but tend to be the farm workers and day laborers working for the landowners. Not a middle class as we think of it, but a sharp contrast between the "haves" and the "have nots."

This is why much of Jesus' teaching involved social justice issues like paying the laborer his wage, not holding back what he earned that day. He challenged the ruling class to invite the poor to their table for a meal. He assured the poor that as God took care of the birds He would see that they had food. This is why when the five thousand came to hear Him preach and heal them, they had nothing to eat at the end of the day...they were poor.

Jesus did not play favorites with the poor, but understood that they were more hungry and receptive to His message than the self-satisfied upper classes. And so it is today. The gospel is growing in the southern hemisphere of poorer nations while it withers in wealthier European countries that once had a great heritage of faith.

Some of my richest overseas trips have been to Uganda, building homes for orphaned children. We join the Christian community in these countries to bless their people, but always come away more humbled and filled by them than anything we gave out.

I need the poor to keep my needs in perspective and my hope in the things that really matter. Serving alongside my fellow ministers who live and work in the city is humbling and gratifying, all at the same time. They appreciate my friendship and the resources my church and I can bring, while we are inspired by their courage, sacrifice and love. I always receive more than I give.

Please note that choosing to serve the poor as a spiritual discipline is different than doing an occasional mission trip or work project. These church-sponsored projects are necessary and led by God, but they are typically not very relational. The joy of serving the poor is really found in the ongoing relationships that we build with the community, whether it's filling a food pantry or preaching in the jails. Mentoring at-risk youth is a huge need and great opportunity to serve Jesus as they serve "the least of these."

I don't serve the poor because I am so godly and self-sacrificing; on the contrary, I am selfish and comfort-oriented and, if left to my own devices, would isolate myself from the pain and needs of others.

The whole point of the disciplines is to say "no" to my flesh and take up the cross/cause/mission of Jesus so that I can walk in the flow of the Holy Spirit. The disciplines always feel hard and unnatural at first, but become sweet and a joy as we grow in grace. I am not earning God's favor, but putting myself in a place where I can hear God and see Him at work. It is in places of need and deprivation where the Kingdom of God is most visible. I need the poor for my soul's sake.

Some may think that practicing the spiritual disciplines has just come back in vogue, but that is only because we have gotten smarter than Jesus. Our Lord lived by and modeled these habits from the opening pages of the Gospel of Mark right through to Gethsemane.

No passage more clearly presents the need for the disciplines than Jesus' declaration in Mark 8:34: *If anyone wishes to come after Me, he must deny himself* (say "no" to what comes naturally and say "yes" to what Jesus wants from me) *and take up his cross and follow Me* (identify with Jesus, practicing the habits of life and mission that Jesus modeled for us).

May we find the joy of following Jesus in these practices, and may we lead others to do the same. This is the way of the transformed life we are longing to experience.

Discussion Questions

1. Which disciplines have you incorporated in your walk with Christ? Do you tend to gravitate toward those that come more naturally, or those that are more challenging? (This is not a loaded question, just curious.)

2. How successful have you been with implementing times of solitude into your schedule? What is the greatest challenge to making this a priority?

3. What has been your history with memorizing Scripture? Do you have a plan in place? It is always easier to do with a group than alone.

4. What do you think about the idea of serving the poor as a discipline? Do you have some experience in this regard?

Worship which does not produce
witness is hypocrisy.

(Dr. Joe Aldrich, *Lifestyle Evangelism*)

Chapter 7
Evangelism Rarely Happens in the Church Pew

Although I was raised in a church-going family, attending church was not on my list of fun things to do when I went to college. If Christ was going to find me (and I am convinced that He finds us) He would have to use someone in my world – and He did. One Sunday morning, as I was recovering from too much fraternity life style the night before, I was led to Christ by a fraternity brother in my frat dorm. The next Thursday at 3:00 a.m., having spent hours talking about what just happened to me last Sunday, I led my girlfriend Margie (now my wife of 34 years) to Christ.

My best friend at the time, John, was living in a house off campus. So I went and shared Jesus with him, only to be rebuffed and lovingly mocked about my new "crutch." He was later led to the Lord by some high school students in the drama class he was teaching. I will never forget John calling me at 1:00 a.m. while I was in seminary to tell me he had prayed the prayer in that funny little booklet I gave him (The Four Spiritual Laws). Today he is a preacher and speaker for the gospel of God.

Notice what is missing from all three conversion stories? A church service. Whether it's the seeker service or the altar call, we still can't seem to shake the idea that the worship service is where Jesus does His best saving work. I'm not sure if we have gotten smarter than Jesus (or lazier) on this one, but there is no missing the point that Jesus takes His message on the road to homes and work places and weddings and parties. He doesn't expect the lost and the outcast to come to the synagogue to hear Him. He goes to them, and it is time we did the same. It is more fun, and much more effective.

The classic passage in this regard is Mark 2:14-17. Jesus has passed by Levi's tax booth and invited him to join His band of disciples, to follow Him. It appears that Levi has been waiting and hoping the invitation would come, for he immediately gets up and throws a party at his home in honor of Jesus. As Mark tells us, there were many tax collectors and irreligious or "unchurched" Jews also at the party...sinners! And if you have been to a party of people who don't know Jesus, you know their behavior can be risky for a believer's reputation. That is exactly what happens to Jesus.

The local legalists, scribes and Pharisees are quick to point out how badly this reflects on Jesus (as if they were really concerned about his reputation), asking His disciples: *Why is He eating and drinking with tax collectors and sinners?* (Mark 2:16).

The fact that no response is recorded by the disciples tells me the legalists had them flat-footed on this one. To be honest, they were not sure why the Messiah would hang with such questionable characters, either. They were still learning this grace and mercy value, themselves. So Jesus sets them straight: *It is not those who are healthy who need a physician, but those who are sick; I did not come to call the righteous, but sinners* (Mark 2:17).

I am so glad that Jesus did not wait for me to go to church to save me, or that my fraternity brother did not try to drag me to church on Sunday morning. I would never have gone. Fortunately, Jeff had been trained by a campus ministry to be praying for his lost friends and to look for opportunities to share the gospel at the frat or wherever it made sense to talk about Jesus.

> *I am so glad that Jesus did not wait for me to go to church to save me, or that my fraternity brother did not try to drag me to church on Sunday morning. I would never have gone.*

Doing Evangelism the Way Jesus Did

I am calling for leaders of our churches to reclaim Sunday morning for preaching the Word to believers and worshiping the Living God without apology or concern for unbelievers.

I once pastored a church with a seeker-oriented service on Sunday morning. That is a service designed to present the claims of Christ in an entertaining format, with popular music and a sketch to bring home the point. Great musicians, lots of humor, and an engaging and topical message. After surveying about two thousand attendees of both the seeker service and the worship services, we found that the strongest factor in getting unchurched people to come to either format was the invitation of a believing friend. The same survey showed us that those invited by a friend were more likely to make a decision for Christ and become part of our church than those who wandered in on their own.

We have put too much confidence in the "Field of Dreams" philosophy of evangelism... "If we build it they will come." (Remember that movie with Kevin Costner as the farmer who built the baseball diamond in his cornfield?) We have become passive about the greatest news a person could ever hear, hoping they will show up at our church on Sunday morning. Some still do, probably because they have a church background and know where to look. But our culture is quickly moving away from any kind of church background. The seeking person is more likely to visit a tattoo parlor or coffee shop on Sunday for some solace and inspiration before attending a church.

So it's time to do evangelism the way Jesus did, by spending time with lost people where they live and hang out. It is time to intentionally get involved in the lives of our neighbors for their souls' sake, that we might earn a hearing for the good news of Jesus.

Two of my staff men coach football as volunteers in our community, one at the high school level and another for elementary age boys. They are clear about their values and have even brought prayer to the team as it was appropriate. Families have investigated our church as a result of the relationship with these staff guys. The key is that they made genuine friendships with these families and earned the right talk about spiritual things.

Researchers continue to point out that most new believers lose touch with their lost friends within three years of their conversion.

Researchers continue to point out that most new believers lose touch with their lost friends within three years of their conversion. This indicates that they are also losing touch with Jesus after three years, because if we are following Jesus we will have a growing love and concern for lost people.

Has your calendar filled up with church-related activities and time with Christians? My greatest occupational hazard is to become isolated from people outside the church while I disciple and pastor believers. I've got to remember that I cannot take people where I have never been. If I want my congregation to be sharing life with unsaved friends, I must model what I preach.

When I first came to Christ, I quickly recognized the Pharisees as the bad guys in the black hats. I saw myself as a young and naive but passionate disciple, and so I related to the twelve and their challenges to grasp who Jesus was and where He was taking them. Now after thirty some years of being a Christian and a pastor, I must face the truth—the Pharisees most likely describe me. I have my pet prejudices about the Bible, ministry, who is doing it right and who is not. I am prone to self-righteousness and critiquing the lifestyle choices of others. I can be proud of my knowledge of the Word and dismiss those who don't know as much. I often act like a Pharisee, and Pharisees are lousy at evangelism! They are good at producing more of their own kind, which is the problem in our churches. You see, the Pharisees thought they were smarter than Jesus.

People today are hungry for integrity. The shattering of our financial system is yet another reason for the common man to question what those in authority are really up to. When they see us investing our resources on campuses designed to "wow" the unchurched to come and check us out, the thoughtful seekers wonder how we can justify so much money spent on ourselves. When we try to play their music, speak their jargon, and be as casual as possible to make them feel at home, they are disappointed by our attempts to be different. I find that the genuine seeking person expects me and my church to be different from the culture. In fact, he is hoping so! That is why he or she is seeking something better than the hollow thrills and ambitions of godless America.

Ultimately, Jesus does the calling and saving. I am invited to join my Lord in the great adventure of fishing for men, but He is the sovereign One working in the hearts of individuals to draw them to Himself. If I am not available to be used for this great privilege, Jesus will find someone who is.

Discussion Questions

1. How were you led to saving faith in Jesus? What role did a local church play in the process? How does your tradition view evangelism? Whose responsibility is it?

2. If you had just fifteen minutes to share with an interested person what it means to know and follow Jesus, what would you say?

3. What is the biggest obstacle for you when it comes to talking to people about your faith?

4. What is your circle of influence (people you love) where you could make inroads for the cause of Christ?

My Passion

Now is the time for men and women to follow Jesus with all their heart, soul, mind and strength to do ministry the way Jesus did, with His priorities and His tools. Are you alarmed as I am that a new generation of young believers is on the brink of throwing out the methodologies of past generations without consideration for what is wheat and what is chaff? My goal in this book is to identify the wheat, that we might continue (or go back to) doing ministry the way Jesus did. The question is not What *Would* Jesus Do, but What *Did* Jesus Do? Unless we are smarter than Jesus, we'll do that.

I have found great freedom of heart and mind by choosing to not play to the crowd, as tempting as that can be to build a successful looking ministry. Again, Jesus is my mentor and model.

As we follow Jesus to the end of the Gospel of Mark, we see Him deserted by the masses when He fails to give them what they want. The cries of "Hosanna" quickly turn to "Crucify him" when He does not overturn the Roman oppressors upon His entry into Jerusalem.

The point is that the masses consistently miss the truth about Jesus. Due to the twisted nature of man because of sin, most people will not want Jesus on His terms. He calls us to believe and follow. He tells us that following will be hard, but worth it. We need to be illuminated by the Spirit of God to understand our need for a savior. Only those who truly see Him for who He is will want to follow Him. And it's our privilege to introduce them to the authentic Jesus whenever we have a chance.

We do people no favor when we convince them that they love Jesus when they really don't. It's dishonest to present the gospel as something that can be added on or fit in nicely with their current life style. The truth is that the genuinely converted recognize their sin and want to repent, to change and follow Him.

If we have to convince people to repent and follow Jesus, we may be trying to coerce goats into acting like sheep.

If we have to convince people to repent and follow Jesus we may be trying to coerce goats into acting like sheep. The loving thing to do is to let the goats know they need Jesus and b alongside when the Spirit of God begins to move on their hearts and open their eyes to their need for Him.

Authenticity, humility and conviction are what genuine seekers of God are looking for. Programs and events have a limited shelf-life, but men and women following the Savior, doing ministry in His power with His priorities will have results of Biblical proportions.

The truth is that none of us really know the full impact we are having in the lives of our people. My hope is that we will forego the quick fix of measuring our lives and ministries by external standards and trust that God will honor work done His way with His tools.

Let's trust Jesus that preaching the Word, gathering to pray, and making disciples is still the best way to do ministry. Let's not get smarter than our Lord. He may just know what He is doing!

To the glory of the King and His Kingdom!

Intermedia Publishing Group

Publishing That Works For You

Do you need a speaker?

Do you want Sandy Mason to speak to your group or event? Then contact Larry Davis at: **(623) 337-8710** or email: **ldavis@intermediapr.com** or use the contact form at: **www.intermediapr.com**.

Whether you want to purchase bulk copies of *Smarter than Jesus?* or buy another book for a friend, get it now at: **www.imprbooks.com**.

If you have a book that you would like to publish, contact Terry Whalin, Publisher, at Intermedia Publishing Group, (623) 337-8710 or email: twhalin@intermediapub. com or use the contact form at: www.intermediapub.com.